CHURCH LEADERSHIP

CHURCH LEADERSHIP

VISION
TEAM
CULTURE
AND
INTEGRITY

Lovett H. Weems, Jr.

FOREWORD BY ROSABETH MOSS KANTER
PROFESSOR, HARVARD BUSINESS SCHOOL

Abingdon Press
Nashville

CHURCH LEADERSHIP: VISION, TEAM, CULTURE, INTEGRITY

Copyright © 1993 by Abingdon Press

This book is printed on acid-free, recycled paper.

Library of Congress Cataloging-in-Publication Data

Weems, Lovett H. (Lovett Hayes)
  Church leadership : vision, team, culture, integrity / Lovett H. Weems, Jr.
    p.   cm.
  Includes bibliographical references.
  ISBN 0-687-13341-6 (alk paper)
  1. Christian leadership. 2. Clergy—Office.   I. Title.
BV652.1.W44   1993
262'.1—dc20   93-18119
                                                                      CIP

Scripture quotations noted NRSV are from the New Revised Standard Version Bible, Copyright © 1989 by the Division of Christian Education of the National Council of the Churches of Christ in the USA. Used by permission.

Those noted JB are from *The Jerusalem Bible,* copyright © 1966 by Darton, Longman & Todd, Ltd. and Doubleday, a division of Bantam Doubleday Dell Publishing Group, Inc. Reprinted by permission of the publishers.

Those noted NEB are from *The New English Bible.* © The Delegates of the Oxford University Press and The Syndics of the Cambridge University Press 1961, 1970. Reprinted by permission.

Those noted KJV are from the King James Version of the Bible.

Material quoted from *The Art of Innovation* by Rosabeth Moss Kanter is used by permission of Nightingale-Conant Corporation, 1-800-525-9000.

93 94 95 96 97 98 99 00 01 02—10 9 8 7 6 5 4 3 2 1

MANUFACTURED IN THE UNITED STATES OF AMERICA

To Saint Paul School of Theology Colleagues

The faculty, staff, students,
friends, graduates, and trustees
who demonstrate each day
the meaning of roving leadership

CONTENTS

CONTENTS

ACKNOWLEDGMENTS

My special indebtedness to those associated with Saint Paul School of Theology is reflected in the dedication. It is out of the mission of Saint Paul that this issue, research, teaching, and writing have emerged. Students in both the Practice of Leadership course and the Advanced Leadership Seminar have added much through their questions and contributions. Advice and guidance from a superb faculty have enriched my study. Suggestions and encouragement from staff and trustees have been invaluable. All of these are colleagues to whom I look as my leaders in so many ways. While not directly related to this writing project, a grant to Saint Paul School of Theology from the Teagle Foundation in New York City has made possible key components of the leadership emphasis at Saint Paul. Richard W. Kimball, Teagle president, has been a probing and supportive partner over these past years.

Denominational leaders have given of their time and ideas generously. I am grateful to clergy colleagues with whom I have the privilege to work and from whom I have learned. Laity in the local churches I served over an eighteen-year period and those with whom I work now have helped me understand what is both right and wrong with leadership in the church.

As you will see in what follows, many of my insights have come from my family, a family that has participated in and been shaped by the leadership of the church. My spouse, Emily, and I are beneficiaries of the ministry of the church, and we hope for vital church leadership for our children—Lovett III, Dee, Elizabeth, and Lawrence—and for all the children of the church.

Special thanks go to Susan Sonnenday Vogel, Executive Vice-President of Saint Paul School of Theology. Her able oversight of the day-to-day work of the seminary makes possible my research, teaching, and writing. In addition, she and I now team-teach the Practice of Leadership course. Her editorial and substantive contributions to this manuscript are monumental. Thanks also go to Kimberly Neilon-Boyd, Administrative Assistant in the President's Office, who may know this manuscript better than anyone else after working with it so diligently for the last two years.

FOREWORD

Is there a single institution today that is not preoccupied with revitalization and renewal? Is there an organization that does not need leaders who can cope with and produce change?

Throughout the world, institutions of all kinds face almost unprecedented pressures for change—whether governments, businesses, hospitals, schools, or churches. Their citizens or customers or clients or congregations are less automatically loyal, less willing to accept what is offered or do what they are told without question, and more demanding of a voice in decisions. Indeed, because institutions have sometimes promised more than they can deliver, their very credibility is at stake.

Thus, institutions in every sector are worrying about their futures, rethinking their ways of working, and seeking leaders who can make a difference.

The task of leadership *is* change. Leaders inspire others to their best efforts in order to do better, to attain higher purposes. Leaders are not satisfied with the status quo. They are not satisfied with maintaining things as they are. They are idealists who believe that things can be better, utopians who dream of perfection. Leaders, therefore, must be change masters. They must understand how to create and guide innovation.

Change masters journey through three stages. First, they formulate a vision that gives direction to people's hopes and desires. Imagination and courage are essential. To inspire people to seek a new destination requires a picture of what is possible, and creating that picture is an act of imagination. Leaders have to challenge conventional wisdom, and stretch their own thinking to go beyond the limits of what already *is* to imagine what *could be.*

But finding a better way can seem impossible to people who have never thought of themselves as capable of doing things differently. All innovations, however wonderful in retrospect, sound like impossible dreams at first. The visions that leaders create must also give people the faith and confidence that the dream is attainable—by them. Leaders, therefore, are cheerleaders who applaud people's capabilities, who show people that they are competent.

Next, change masters need the power to advance their idea by selling people, involving people, influencing people to invest their own time, energy, and resources in realizing the vision. What makes leaders effective is their ability to mobilize a set of backers and supporters who also believe in the vision. Coalitions like this are especially important for the work of change. Change requires resources and expertise above and beyond what is necessary for the status quo. It meets with inevitable resistance, requiring champions that can advocate the vision and satisfy critics.

Coalition building not only attracts needed power to a new effort, but it also helps guarantee success. Once others are brought in and contribute their money or support to a project, they also have a stake in making it work. Their egos and reputations are now on the line. And, of course, very few ideas are implemented by one person alone. The efforts of many people are necessary to carry out the specific tasks that must be done if a vision is to be realized.

Finally, change masters must maintain the momentum, keeping faith and hope alive during the hard and sometimes frustrating work of execution and implementation. Many things inevitably go wrong in the course of making changes or leading people in a new direction. Or the journey toward the destination simply takes longer than imagined, and people get weary from the work. In my research on innovation I discovered a basic truth of leadership, if not of life: "Everything looks like a failure in the middle."

If leaders give up when they hit the first obstacle to the dream, then by definition all the effort they have put in has brought nothing. But if they persist and persevere—learning from mistakes, redirecting effort where necessary, urging people onward, celebrating minor victories along the way—then they are likely to succeed. Leadership is an act of commitment. Leaders should not start things that they are not willing to complete. And they must stay personally involved—while turning over more and more of the power to act to the larger group of people they have involved.

Lovett Weems's interactive approach to leadership recognizes the importance of the relationship between leaders and followers. Leadership does not exist within a person; it resides in the relationship between persons. Leaders are defined by the power their followers lend them. Followers, in turn, are empowered by leaders to do more than they ever imagined.

Dr. Weems has provided an invaluable guide to leadership in the church, one well suited to produce more change masters. But do churches need change masters, some wonder? Some people do not want religious institutions to change. They equate the religious mission of promulgating values rooted in long historical traditions with the concrete buildings, organization charts, and practices invented by previous generations.

Dr. Weems thinks the distinction between continuity and change is a false one. He writes, "The only way to preserve values over time is to be involved continuously in renewal and change, thus finding ever fresh expressions for those values. When any organization decides it will seek to save its life by building walls against change, that organization is destined to lose its life, its vitality."

This is a powerful message. The best way for institutions to endure and prosper is to encourage leaders who will build on the past by envisioning an even better future.

Rosabeth Moss Kanter is professor of business administration at Harvard University's Business School. Recently she coauthored *The Challenge of Organizational Change: How Companies Experience It and Leaders Guide It.*

PREFACE

Like good stewards of the manifold grace of God, serve one another with whatever gift each of you has received.

1 Peter 4:10 NRSV

In 1959 Henry Pitney Van Dusen, president of Union Theological Seminary in New York City, spoke at the inauguration of Don W. Holter, the first president of Saint Paul School of Theology. He described the state of the church and religion just over thirty years ago.

Clearly, the most significant feature, as it is the most striking feature, of our "present situation" is what a popular journal of wide circulation recently captioned: THE CURRENT BOOM IN RELIGION. . . . As the author of that article, Dr. Eugene Carson Blake, summarizes the evidence: "Yes, the boom is upon us. Call it what you will—a religious resurgence, a move back to God, a reawakening—it's here." The diagnosis is confirmed by a more objective authority. Perhaps the most astute European observer of the American scene, Professor D. W. Brogan of Cambridge University, recently wrote: "Religion in the United States, like many other things, is booming . . . that there is a genuine religious revival, I do not doubt. That the churches are not in retreat, I do not doubt."

14

Now contrast that description with the 1989 article by Richard N. Ostling in *Time* magazine, which pointed out that in the last two decades five mainline denominations had a net loss of 5.2 million members, while the population of the country rose 47 million. The figures are even worse when one looks at people of color and people in poverty.

Through the years, those within and outside the church have described both good and difficult times. In his novel *Light in August*, William Faulkner wrote: "That which is destroying the church is not the outward groping of those within it or the inward groping of those without, but the professionals who control it and who have removed the bells from its steeples." Many are listening for their pastors to ring out a clear and sure message of faith and hope.

There is a hunger for a compelling message and commitment to an essential mission. People are weary of what G. K. Chesterton called cures that don't cure, blessings that don't bless, and solutions that don't solve.

THE LEADERSHIP CHALLENGE

It is in this current, challenging situation that the church calls its pastors to exercise effective leadership. Harris W. Lee examined leadership studies over the past fifty years and learned that there are at least 350 definitions of leadership. His study led him to affirm James MacGregor Burns's conclusion that leadership is "one of the most observed and least understood phenomena on earth." Similarly, when Ralph Stodgill had completed his examination of several thousand books and articles, he wrote: "Four decades of research on leadership have produced a bewildering mass of findings. . . . It is difficult to know what, if anything, has been convincingly demonstrated by replicated research. The endless accumulation of empirical data has not produced an integrated understanding of leadership."[1]

Leadership is difficult to define. "Leadership has an elusive, mysterious quality about it," says David P. Campbell of the Center for Creative Leadership. "It is easy to recognize, difficult to practice, and almost impossible to create in others on demand.

Perhaps no other topic has created as much attention from observers, participants and philosophers—with so little agreement as to the basic facts."[2]

Thomas E. Cronin, McHugh professor of American Institutions and Leadership at Colorado College, acknowledges that "effective leadership remains in many ways the most baffling of the performing arts. There is an element of mystery about it. Intuition, flare, risk-taking, and sometimes even theatrical ability come into play. And leadership needs vary from organization to organization, culture to culture. There is no set formula."

Leaders come in all sizes, shapes, and colors, and with varying dispositions, Cronin says. Some talk a lot and some are more reflective. Some are reserved, while others are charismatic. Some lead from within, while others organize movements. "Leadership," Cronin concludes, "is hard to define and even harder to quantify because it is part purpose, part process, and part product; part the why and part the how; part the artistic and intuitive and only part the managerial."[3]

While virtually impossible to define precisely, leadership is almost universally recognized. Bishop Rueben P. Job is right—"Ask any local congregation and they will tell you when they see it and when they don't."

Thus in an extremely difficult and challenging environment, we ask pastors and church leaders today to exercise what we can hardly define. "Leaders in all fields," contends consultant Gary H. Quehl, "must operate in an environment that defies rational order and prediction." Quehl uses Peter Vaill's metaphor of "permanent white water" to describe leaders being asked to play a game no one knows how to play anymore: "Paradox, ambiguity, and contradiction are the dominant characteristics of our white water environment."

What Quehl is saying about higher education is equally true for church leadership today. Both face Vaill's Grand Paradox of Management: We ask leaders to take responsibility for controlling what is less and less controllable. As our environment becomes more unstable and less predictable, the paradox intensifies. Leadership becomes more important than management, because it takes a leader to invent strategies to improve our organization's adaptation to present and future circumstances.[4]

16

LEADERSHIP AS STEWARDSHIP

Nevertheless, pastors are leaders, and the importance of the calling by the church to leadership takes on even greater significance in difficult times. As Robert R. Blake and Jane S. Mouton propose, "In the final analysis, leadership is everything."[5] The best of message, opportunity, resources, facilities, and people will count for little if leadership falters and is ineffective.

Perhaps the greatest paradox, but the most hopeful promise, is that whatever else leadership may be, for the Christian church it always remains a gift from God. It is a treasure in clay jars. "Not that we are competent of ourselves to claim anything as coming from us; our competence is from God, who has made us competent to be ministers of a new covenant" (2 Corinthians 3:5-6a NRSV).

Leadership, like other work of the people of faith, depends upon the vigorous and responsible use of the talents God has given to each of us. It depends upon the work of the Spirit weaving those talents into a rich tapestry. It is the marvelous and mysterious working of God through our lives and work that we call grace. Leadership is a gift from God, confirmed by the church, for the service of others and the upbuilding of the body of Christ.

Leadership is in essence a ministry of stewardship. It is through the proper stewardship of purpose, time, resources, opportunities, challenges, and energies of the people of God that vital ministry and mission take place. Leaders are indeed "good stewards of the manifold grace of God."

INTRODUCTION

If you are a leader, exert yourself to lead.

Romans 12:8*b* NEB

Leadership is needed for Christian communities as for other human communities, but not necessarily leadership in a fixed hierarchical model. Churches are likely to grow toward partnership among their members when there is a dynamic of leadership behavior among a variety of people and not just one leader.

Letty M. Russell, *The Future of Partnership*

My personal interest in the subject of leadership emerged from two experiences during my first two years as a seminary president.

Feeling that I needed to listen before speaking, immediately upon becoming president of Saint Paul I began to have conversations with many people. I met with clergy leaders, but most of the conversations were with groups of laypeople, those who are the ultimate beneficiaries or victims of what happens in seminary. I listened and took notes. I was learning from these conversations from the beginning; but after two years I thought back in a special way over the many conversations I had had with laity across the church during those months. I asked myself, "What are they saying about ministry that we in the seminary need to hear?"

The first thing was easy and obvious—preaching. No subject is more on laypersons' minds than preaching as they think of the preparation of persons for ministry. The subject came up in every discussion I had with laity. But there was something else in every conversation. I missed it for over a year, partly because the people were not using traditional seminary language, and partly because they may not have been sure exactly how to state their concern. If I had to put the issue into one word it would be "leadership." Sometimes laity talk about the desire for spiritual leadership from the pastor. Sometimes they talk about moral standards in leadership. It comes out in calls for administrative leadership. I saw it in their desire for worship leadership, and in the cry throughout the church for strong pastoral leadership.

The second key experience that brought me to a concern for leadership came during those same years as I preached in a different church nearly every Sunday. It is amazing how much one can learn and sense about the spirit and vitality of a congregation within a short time. I imagine church visitors have that experience every Sunday. It took only a matter of months for me to come to realize that the pastor was the key variable from church to church. And it did not matter whether the pastor was male or female, young or old, liberal or conservative, or a graduate of one seminary or another. The key difference was to be found in whether the pastor was a leader and exercising pastoral leadership.

Do not hear this as a call for an autocratic style of leadership. Laypeople do not want that; they will not permit it. However, the pastor is a leader, and the first task of a leader is to lead. People of the church want and expect strong and compelling, as well as open and collegial, leadership from the pastor.

STATE OF LEADERSHIP TODAY

In November 1987, a cover story in *Time* magazine asked the question, "Who's in charge?" They answered their own question with these discouraging words, "The nation calls for leadership, and there is no one home." Or as the *New York Times* headline two days before the 1988 presidential election read, "People are Yearning for a Leader, but Expecting Much Less."

The historian James MacGregor Burns in his pivotal book, *Leadership,* says, "One of the most universal cravings of our time is a hunger for compelling and creative leadership."[1] More recently in an interview on the "MacNeil/Lehrer Newshour" he said that we "live in a time of mediocre leadership politically and intellectually, and that profoundly disturbs me."[2] Robert K. Greenleaf's work on the concept of servant leadership has been extremely helpful for many people. "The leadership crisis of our time," he says, "is without precedent."[3]

Cornel West of Princeton University, writing after the 1992 Los Angeles riots, spoke of the "paucity of courageous leadership" and said "the major challenge is the need to generate new leadership. . . . We need leaders . . . who can situate themselves within a larger historical narrative of this country and world, who can grasp the complex dynamics of our peoplehood and imagine a future grounded in the best of our past, yet attuned to the frightening obstacles that now perplex us."[4]

Another thoughtful observer and writer, the educator and public servant John W. Gardner, spoke years ago about an "antileadership vaccine" in America. He believes that we are in danger of destroying the effectiveness of those who have a natural gift for leadership, and that we are not doing what we should to encourage potential leaders. "We are immunizing a high proportion of our most gifted young people against any tendencies to leadership."[5]

NECESSITY OF LEADERSHIP

Religious educator Sara Little has observed that "whenever crises have been met or clear vision has pulled people together with a sense of collective identity and an articulated purpose that replaces fumbling hopelessness, it seems that often, almost always, some leader—a prophet, a martyr, an organizer who knows how to give form to vision and words to yearnings of the heart, a person embodying courage—has had a hand in what happened."[6]

No organization can function without leadership. "The failure . . . to take charge and give active leadership," according to former Harvard professor Harry Levinson, "can be as devastating to an organization as frankly autocratic leadership."[7] Gardner puts it this way, "In our democratic society, we make grants of power to people for specified purposes. If for ideological or temperamental reasons they refuse to exercise the power granted, we must turn to others."[8]

When Douglas McGregor left his faculty position at MIT to become president of Antioch College, he had reservations about the appropriateness of leaders taking an activist role within an organization. When leaving the college presidency to return to teaching, he reflected on his change of mind in this way: "I couldn't have been more wrong. It took a couple of years, but I finally began to realize that a leader cannot avoid the exercise of authority anymore than [the leader] can avoid responsibility for what happens to one's organization."[9]

"We can have the kinds of leaders we want," says Gardner, "but we cannot choose to do without them."[10]

TEN OBSERVATIONS ABOUT LEADERSHIP

1. Leadership needs to be demythologized.

We need to take much of the mystery out of the subject of leadership. For example, some feel that leaders are born, while it is clear today that most of the skills of leadership can be learned. Some associate leadership with a particular type of personality; yet leaders have all different types of personalities, just as they are male and female, young and old, from all national, racial, ethnic, and cultural backgrounds.

People too often think of a leader as the solo leader, when most effective leadership involves a team. People associate leadership and power in a way that is often oversimplified. As a study of college presidents pointed out, leaders such as presidents have far more power than they think, but much less power than others tend to think they have.[11] The power of leaders is never a generic power, but always a power related to interrelationships with others.

2. Leadership is not simple.

While this book attempts to make leadership as neat, orderly, and understandable as possible, one needs always to remember that leadership is hardly neat, orderly, and understandable. Leadership is extremely complex and ambiguous. Leadership is filled more with frustration and joy than with order and clarity.

Michael D. Cohen and James G. March have concluded that both observers and practitioners "underestimate the complexity of leadership processes and situations and overestimate the significance of individual leaders."[12] "Part of my excitement in living," says Greenleaf, "comes from the belief that leadership is so dependent on spirit that the essence of it will never be capsuled or codified."[13]

3. Leadership is spiritual.

Leadership and the spirit are closely related. Leadership is a spiritual experience and endeavor.

Leadership is not a science, even if it appears to be at times. The more one works at leadership, studies leadership, and gains experience in leadership, the better leader one will be. But the effective leader relies not so much on effort, education, or experience, but on judgment, feeling, sense, values, and intuition. In essence, we are talking about a kind of discernment one can only understand in spiritual terms.

4. Leadership is about group purpose.

Leadership is always for people and group purpose. Leadership never occurs in a vacuum, but always within an organization, a group, a community, a context. A church leader of another era liked to say that a locomotive can go faster by itself, but the task of the locomotive is to pull a train. This is the task of a leader. Helen Doohan in her study, *Leadership in Paul*, points out that Paul's leadership was enhanced not only by his ability to assess a situation correctly, but also by his ability to listen and to be perceived as a servant of the community.[14]

5. Leadership is chaotic.

Someone has observed that for leaders, much of the time most things are out of control. One of Terry Deal's marvelous definitions of leadership is that the task of the leader is "the ability to be out of control comfortably."

Cohen and March described the life of the college president as "organized anarchy" because it is characterized by problematic goals, unclear technology, and fluid participation. The title of their study, *Leadership and Ambiguity*, reflects not only that ambiguity is the dominant characteristic for leadership for college presidents, but that it is also a primary characteristic for all leadership.

For leaders life is never simple, and important issues are never all settled at once. Those who require this type of orderliness in their lives need to find vocations requiring only administration and management. It may appear to observers within and outside an organization that things are going well. The effective leader, however, is much closer to the mission of the organization and its current reality, and so will identify new and potentially problematic issues to keep the group moving toward the mission.

6. Leadership is funny.

It is almost impossible to consider the possibility of an effective leader who does not have a working sense of humor. Leadership is funny. To be so serious that one misses the humor in it, especially that which comes as a result of and at the expense of the leader, is a great loss. Without a sense of humor, the leader not only misses an important element of leadership, but also misses the release that humor brings.

7. Most research about leadership is not taking place in the church.

Most of the best research and writing on leadership in recent years has not been done in the context of the church or not-for-profit institutions. Those in business have done most of this work, followed by those in politics and government. Today there is an increasing interest in the subject of leadership in the not-for-profit arena and, one would hope, much of this can be done in the church.

Much of the research has been done in recent years and has the advantage of being up-to-date, but its newness does not give opportunity to compare with data over a long period of time.

Another bias in the research is that most of it has been extremely limited in racial and gender inclusiveness. Studies about racial/ethnic persons and women are not totally missing from the research, but their representation is limited. The literature on women in leadership is beginning to grow much more rapidly and is showing both key similarities and differences from studies that were done primarily with men. Remarkably, many contemporary learnings about leadership were reflected originally in a book on business administration, *Dynamic Administration,* written by Mary Parker Follett in 1941. It was apparently the first book on administration by an American woman to be published.[15]

8. Any learning about leadership is only a beginning.

In this book we will be covering basic theory, concepts, and findings about effective leadership. What you gain from this and other resources should be seen as a beginning of a lifelong education in leadership. I once thought that a time would come when I would know all I needed to know about administration, management, and leadership. Then I would shift my attention to carrying out what I had learned. Not so.

Leadership is far more of an adventure than that. It is much more dynamic than static. One should have as a goal to make some new discovery about one's own work in leadership every day.

One way that this takes place is through an ongoing interplay in your mind between theory and experience. Learning good theory out of the study of the experience of others can and should shape and change how you do your work. Similarly, your own experiences will come to give you insights into theory about leadership that will guide and direct you. For instance, before I ever read one study on leadership, I had developed theories about how change takes place within the local church that grew out of my eighteen years as a local pastor. These theories were simple and unsophisticated, but they have turned out to match quite well the findings on leadership and change as it takes place in almost any type of organization. We need to take theory very seriously but we also need to take seriously our learnings from experience.

Leadership includes a lifelong journey filled with continuing growth. Leaders are people with a capacity to grow, who thrive on challenge and new experiences, and who are excited about the possibilities of new learnings and change.

9. Leadership is an art.

Max DePree, Chair and CEO of Herman Miller, Inc., has written an intriguing book entitled *Leadership Is an Art.* In it he says that "leadership is much more an art, a belief, a condition of the heart, than a set of things to do."[16] The more one learns about leadership, the more one realizes that it is far more an art than a science.

The French painter Braque once said, "The only thing that matters in art can't be explained." Warren Bennis reminds us that the same can be said about leadership. But leadership, like art, can be demonstrated. Leadership is like beauty: it is hard to define, but you know it when you see it. Harry Levinson puts it this way:

> Leadership is an art to be cultivated and developed. Like any other form of art, if it becomes stereotyped it is no longer art but merely a replica. An artistic achievement is varied in texture, composition, symbolism, color. It is dynamic in the eyes of the viewer because it takes on new meaning with each perception. In short, it lives. So it is with the work of the good leader. In different circumstances, at different times, with different problems, leaders choose different modes of action. It is this flexibility, together with a conception of and appreciation for the role, that makes leaders like diamonds—solid, strong, yet many-faceted and therefore sparkling. This is why leadership cannot be learned by prescription or content.[17]

10. Leadership is never an end in itself.

Leadership can never be understood apart from mission and vision. Leadership never exists for itself or for the glorification or even personal development of the leader. Leadership exists to make possible a preferred future (vision) for the people involved, which reflects the heart of the mission and values to which they are committed.

One can manage and administer without a real sense of spiritual direction, but one cannot lead in this manner. One can only lead in relationship to those things for which one can sincerely say, "I have a dream that someday. . . ."

My purpose in writing this book relates to my driving passion—the church and its future. As a seminary president, I spend my time doing many things that go with the calling of that office. As with all leadership, most of the daily activities would appear to the casual observer as routine and ordinary. But behind them is a vision. For me that vision is the revitalization of the church. I hope that through this material on leadership, I can be associated with helping those of you who read it to become extraordinary leaders for the church.

ONE

ELEMENTS OF EFFECTIVE LEADERSHIP

F rom its beginning the church has recognized the need for some persons to be set apart for leadership of the community. The church father Jerome put it, "There can be no church community without a leader or team of leaders."[1] Theologian Annie Jaubert reminds us that in the earliest Christian communities leadership was seen as "the responsibility of all and the charge of some."[2]

The quality, tone, and style of the pastor's leadership are important; none of these factors, however, takes away from the necessity of the leader functioning as a real leader while holding the position of leadership. "Leaders lead," says Kennon Callahan. "Leaders do not manage or administrate, manipulate or dictate, process or enable,—they lead. . . . And the grouping—whether a local church, a subcultural grouping, a movement, or a nation—senses that *this person* is helping them toward discovery and fulfillment."[3]

One way to think about one's leadership role is to ask the question, "What is it for which the church looks to me which, if I do not do it, no one else can or will?" Another way to ask this is, "What is it that the church has a *right* to expect of me? What is it that, if I do not do it, no one else will because they do not have either the position or the preparation to do it?"

Obviously, the pastor is not the only leader in the life of the church. However, within the local church the greatest variable from one church to another is the pastor and the quality of the pastor's leadership. What is said about pastoral leadership is true for the many leaders within the church and leaders in other organizations. The primary focus here is on the leadership role of the pastor. As will become clear in what follows, this role is always seen in relation to other leaders in the church.

James H. Davis and Woodie W. White, in their study of racial transition in the church, point out that "as a rule, a congregation does not outrun its pastor." They do not know of a single instance where a church made a successful transition without the leadership of the pastor. A few congregations replaced the pastor and then moved ahead, but "a congregation does not lead its pastor. Of course, the pastor can achieve nothing alone. . . . But the attitudes and skills of the minister are of crucial importance, particularly at times of greatest change."[4]

THE DILEMMA OF LEADERSHIP IN THE CHURCH

Part of the dilemma in the church comes from our sharing the general antileadership situation of the larger culture. In the words of former Harvard University president Derek Bok, we live in a time of a "greater questioning of traditional values and a diminished confidence in established institutions and the credibility of their leaders."[5] Greenleaf has looked at the issue of leadership in many settings. His findings in observing the church reflected "considerable concern for the present state of leading in churches and for a consequent diminished influence of churches on their members and on society at large."[6] Sara Little's writing on leadership is based more on "anxiety about the fact that things seem to be 'coming apart'" than on a conviction about leadership development as a strategy for meeting the situation. Her work "presupposes a kind of national and religious crisis of purpose, morality, and identity."[7]

The decline of effective leadership is one of the key factors behind the malaise and decline of mainline Protestant churches in the last generation. One reason for the rise of conservative and fundamentalist churches in this era is that mainline denominations have not presented compelling and appealing alternatives. This is a lack of leadership. It means that we are not engaging our identity, the people, and our environment.

We in the seminaries are clearly a part of the problem and must be a part of the solution. However, the ethos of the church has far more effect upon the way ordained and professional ministry is lived out than what happens in the seminaries.

Most of the work on leadership today is in the for-profit arena (with business school professors doing much of the research and writing). A *Business Week* article on graduate business schools said, however, that "of all the criticisms coming from the executive suites, perhaps the harshest concerns the short shrift that B-schools give to promoting effective leadership skills."[8]

If this is the case, what does it say about the church and seminaries? In surveys clergy say they have a great need for administrative and management skills (time management, conflict management, and so on), but clergy have not even identified the larger issue of leadership. We have done a fairly good job in the church in administration and management. We have not addressed the issue of leadership. At least in the business community there is an acknowledgment that there is a crisis that must be addressed. At this point in the church we are not only lacking the skills and literature about leadership required to make changes, but we are also not even asking the right questions. We have not yet focused on the nature of the crisis and a key source of our problem. Why is this the case?

THREE COMMON CONFUSIONS ABOUT LEADERSHIP

Letty Russell, in her quotation at the beginning of the introduction, identifies the critical importance of leadership in the church and also names a common concern about a hierarchical model. During the past several years, as I have been teaching seminary courses and conducting continuing education seminars on leadership, I have found similar concerns and have identified several common confusions.

1. Confusion between leadership and authority

Authority can be given; leadership must be earned. A person can be assigned, selected, or designated for a position, but a person cannot be appointed to leadership. An important degree of authority comes almost automatically with the assumption of a position. Leadership must be earned minute by minute, hour by hour, day by day over many years. While it must be earned slowly, it can be lost very quickly.

The best thing about authority is that it gives one an opportunity to provide leadership. While the capacity for leadership does not come automatically with authority, authority does put one in a position from which leadership is possible. It is similar to having a parking permit at a large urban university, according to leadership consultant Roland Nelson. The permit gives the right to park—if you can find a parking place.

Authority by itself is never enough. While the opportunities given by authority should be recognized, the church leader who relies upon, "I am the pastor" or "I am in charge of music" will soon be in trouble. Leadership is not to be confused with that initial deference and acceptance that go with authority. The person who tries to rely on authority alone, or even primarily, will not be an effective leader. Authority may be given; leadership is ultimately conferred by the people being led. The final test for all leaders is whether someone is following.

Roland Nelson makes the distinction between leadership and authority as it relates to parents. "What my children do while I am around," he says, "is a function of authority. What they do when I am not around is a function of leadership." The moral dimension of leadership is never more apparent than in its relationship to authority.

2. Confusion between leadership and style

One reason some people are reluctant to consider the subject of leadership more seriously is that they have mistakenly come to associate leadership with a particular negative style of leadership. There are various styles of leadership, but no one of them is synonymous with leadership any more than a particular style of teaching is synonymous with education.

Unfortunately, the images we have had regarding leadership

styles have not always been the most helpful, particularly since many describe leadership style in stereotypical terms.

Many have thought of leadership style in terms of a continuum with the authoritarian leader on one end and the laissez-faire leader on the other. The authoritarian pastor is the one who comes into a new church and says, "This is my order of worship." On the other hand, when the laissez-faire pastor is asked about plans for the first worship service upon arrival in a new church, the response is more likely to be, "What do you want?" With the extremes drawn in this way, persons cannot identify with either of those styles, and the temptation is to strike a balance somewhere along the continuum between the extremes.

Another popular image is that of a grid on which the leader's concern for people and concern for the task are indicated. The authoritarian leader is the one who shows total concern for the task and no concern for people. The other extreme—of total concern for what people want, and virtually no concern for the mission—is what Robert R. Blake and Jane S. Mouton have designated on their well-known Managerial Grid as "country club management."[9]

Harry Levinson has written that the failure of persons to provide dynamic and creative leadership today is often "masked by a soft understanding—or misunderstanding—of democratic management." This approach results in a type of management that is not useful either for the people or the mission. Many ministers who see themselves as quite progressive have adopted what is in essence a country club style of management (the members tell me what to do and I do it) more out of reaction to authoritarian style than out of careful reflection upon the options.

A basic problem with both the continuum and the grid images is that they have a hidden and false assumption. People will assume that the more the pastor moves toward an authoritarian model, the stronger the pastor is and the weaker laypeople are; and the more the pastor moves toward a laissez-faire model, the weaker the pastor is and the stronger the laypeople are.

An experience several years ago destroyed this assumption for me. A seminary asked several churches to prepare papers about what they felt should be considered as a curriculum revision took place. They asked one church to participate because the image everyone had of that church was of a "lay-led church." They had a tradition of strong lay leadership that went back over many years. The image of the pastor who served that church, and others who had served the church before him, was primarily of a facilitator who had little to do most of the time. Laypeople from this church submitted a paper that showed that image to be anything but reality. Of all the statements submitted by churches, only theirs referred repeatedly to the pastor. On every page of their document they talked about the key leadership of the pastor.

Here are some examples: "Our pastor led us for a year in the study of the history and meaning of Christian worship so we might together develop our order of worship. . . . Our pastor teaches a Bible study every Wednesday morning. . . . Our pastor encouraged us to become involved with this issue. . . . Our pastor took a group of us to a mission situation to understand more about the problem. . . . Our pastor preached on a particular subject and then gave those interested an opportunity to respond."

This experience caused me to start looking for an alternative way of understanding the relationship between pastor and people that reflected the experience of this church more than does either the continuum or grid model. What I was looking for was a way of leading in which pastor and people are strong together.

What developed was an interactive approach to leadership that simultaneously is attentive to the leader's own identity and values, and is responsive to the needs and interests of others. This approach will be illustrated later. I prefer to speak of it as an approach rather than a style. This interactive approach to leadership can be used by persons with many different personal styles of leadership in a helpful and upbuilding way.

Despite our preoccupation with leadership style, style is not the crucial issue; leadership is. If one measures one's own approach to leadership by the best learnings about what a leader is and what a leader does, then one will discover if there are negative and destructive patterns of leadership. This is a much more helpful approach than beginning with an ideological commitment to a particular style of functioning with little regard for the calling of the leadership position. This interactive approach is offered as a more missional stance for ministry. A missional stance requires us to begin with the unique ministry situation that is ours, not with self. Mission requires more than self-expression and self-fulfillment. To begin with the needs of the setting makes this clear. One will bring many personal character-istics to leadership, all of which, including leadership style, will have to be considered as one seeks to exercise effective leader-ship to meet the needs of the situation.

3. Confusion of leadership with enabling and empowering

Today enabling and empowering are the shorthand ways to talk about leaders not dominating others. The terms are helpful in providing a needed caution against abuse of followers by lead-ers. However, they are not particularly helpful in describing the specific positive tasks required of leaders.

One cannot talk about these terms alone. Enabling and empowering never take place within a vacuum, and they do not convert neatly into a specific way of working without reference to other realities. By themselves they will keep you from abusing a group, but will not necessarily mean that you will provide lead-ership for the group. All too easily they can lead to something like the country club model of leadership where one gets some people together, asks them what they want, writes it on newsprint, and then tries to make sure that it happens. The real result is often inaction because of the leader's fear of moving forward beyond what others may deem appropriate. Even when action does result, it often is insufficiently related to the pressing missional imperatives. Probing questions and pertinent reminders of the group's reason for being are often crucial for a group to stay attuned to its mission.

"The time for leaders has come, the time for enablers has passed," is the admonition of church consultant Kennon L. Callahan. He contends that there may have been a time when it was useful to think of leaders as enablers; the enabler manage-ment philosophy was a major contribution in overcoming the benevolent authoritarian styles of leadership of many pastors and laypersons. But too often church leaders have used the enabler philosophy to avoid sharing their own agenda, direc-tion, and vision straightforwardly, or to manipulate the decision-making process in covert ways. In actual practice, many enablers are not really enablers; they are covert manipulators. They use the techniques of process to manipulate the group toward their own conclusions. Or conversely, the enabler is frequently so faithful to the process that the group does not get the benefit of the enabler's own wisdom, judgment, and common sense. The enabler pastor focuses too much on the process, and not enough on how to achieve the mission. In short, Callahan maintains, local congregations need "more leaders and fewer enablers."[10]

We are seeking a way of leading that will strengthen both pastor and people. The goal is to illustrate an approach to leadership which, if done well, will cause both the pastor and the congregation to feel and be stronger than ever before.

The key is not to focus on a term or process, but on an approach to leadership that takes seriously the values, ideas, dreams, and concerns of both pastor and people. The reality of personal and group empowerment around mission and values is what we seek.

ADMINISTRATION, MANAGEMENT, AND LEADERSHIP

One step in defining leadership is to make distinctions among three words: administration, management, and leadership.

Administration is doing things right. If there is a deadline, one meets it. If there is a prescribed structure, one has it. If there are stated policies, one keeps them.

Management is doing the right things. Management includes such things as long-range planning, goal setting, selecting priorities, time management, and budgeting.

Leadership is the development and articulation of a shared vision, motivation of those key people without whom that vision cannot become a reality, and gaining the cooperation of most of the people involved.

Both administration and management are required for effective leadership. However, administration and management alone do not equal leadership. One can administer and manage without vision and values. It is impossible to lead without vision and values. Leadership is always a moral act. Genuine leadership is always values-driven leadership.

TEACHING LEADERSHIP IN THE CHURCH

Secular literature related to administration grew tremendously in the 1940s and 1950s, particularly after World War II. In those years the church did a good job of converting the best learnings from administration into applications for the life of the church. The same task was done in relationship to the literature of management that exploded in the 1960s and after. Some may say that we have overdone the application of management learnings to the church.

Today there is keen interest in the subject of leadership in many fields, but the church is yet to explore its implications for the life of the church and for the role of ordained leaders within the church. Many in the church tend to devalue, or even look with disdain, on administration, management, and leadership as not relating to the "real ministry" to which the church and its pastors are called. The hope of this book is that pastors and other church leaders will come to see that effective leadership is not only compatible with faithful ministry, it is also essential to the fulfillment of the calling of God to which we have responded.

As we have seen, churches are uncertain about identity and message after twenty-five years of decline and are facing a rapidly changing environment and unpredictable future. In this context, the approaches to leadership growing out of conventional administration and management have proven inadequate. The church desperately needs new wisdom that draws upon the richness of Christian teaching and tradition, and mines the best of contemporary research on leadership. These resources can provide the clues for dynamic church leadership for the critical and decisive years ahead.

What follows are four elements of effective leadership that have emerged from my study of leadership literature and my experience as a local church pastor: vision, team, culture, and integrity.

There are other important dimensions of leadership that are not covered in this volume. Examples include personal characteristics of leaders, gender and leadership, leadership styles, and strategic planning and leadership. These and many other subjects are worthy of thoughtful and serious attention by anyone who would be a leader. This volume, however, addresses the four elements of effective leadership that I believe are the framework within which other leadership issues can be approached and addressed. The following diagram helps visualize these four essential elements of leadership, which will then be explored in the next four chapters.

ELEMENTS OF EFFECTIVE LEADERSHIP

Vision
(Discover and articulate a shared vision.)

Team
(Build the team without whom the vision cannot become a reality.)

Integrity
(Make sure the vision is a reality for the leader[s] and the organization.)

Culture
(Communicate and symbolize the vision throughout the organization's culture.)

TWO

VISION

Where there is no vision, the people perish.

Proverbs 29:18 KJV

The soul . . . never thinks without a picture.

Aristotle

Vision is the single most common theme in leadership studies. A. Bartlett Giamatti's distinction between management and leadership makes this theme clear: "Management is the capacity to handle multiple problems, neutralize various constituencies, motivate personnel. . . . Leadership, on the other hand, is an essentially moral act, not—as in most management—an essentially protective act. It is the assertion of a vision, not simply the exercise of a style."[1] A study of many leaders from different fields of endeavor concluded that "of all the characteristics that distinguished the individuals in this book, the most pivotal was a concern with a guiding purpose, an overarching vision."[2]

> "Cheshire-Puss, . . . would you tell me, please, which way I ought to go from here?"
> "That depends a good deal on where you want to get to," said the Cat.
> "I don't much care where——" said Alice.
> "Then it doesn't matter which way you go," said the Cat.
> "—so long as I get somewhere," Alice added as an explanation.
> "Oh, you're sure to do that," said the Cat, "if you only walk long enough."

Lewis Carroll, *Alice's Adventures in Wonderland*

WHY IS A VISION NECESSARY?

Leadership is about change. It is important to remember that we cannot become what we need to be by remaining what we are. A prayer from the African-American church puts it well, "Lord, we're not what we want to be, we're not what we need to be, we're not what we are going to be, but thank God Almighty, we're not what we used to be."

Change and leadership go together. There can be no real leadership without significant change. For Christians there is a strong theological grounding for change. We must change. The way things are in the world at any moment is never synonymous with God's ultimate will. There is always a "not yet" quality and an incompleteness about things as they are. God is always pulling us into the future with a call for an order far different from the current state of things.

The capacity for perpetuation of an organization, its values, and its mission lies in continuous renewal and regeneration. There is a simple and familiar cycle through which organizations tend to move. The movement is from initial vision to maintenance to decline. In the early days the vision is very pure and the most dominant characteristic of the organization. There is a passion about purpose and mission. Later there comes a time when the organization has taken on many institutional characteristics and thus is able to continue to make significant social impact. However, in this stage there is enough distance from the initial vision that maintenance of the organization comes to the fore and vision often wanes. Cut off from its real source of power (the initial purpose and vision) during this stage, the organization moves into decline.

Is this cycle inevitable? No, but it can change only if there can come moments of recapturing or renewing the vision. In this way a new cycle begins. The new vision is connected to the original vision but is enough of a new manifestation of the vision that renewal is possible.

In the lives of healthy organizations there is an "endless interweaving of continuity and change."[3] The scientist is an example. What appears to us as change and innovation is only possible because the scientist is a part of a tradition and an intellectual system; it is one that provides for its own continuous renewal. The well-known management theorist Peter Drucker maintains that in a world buffeted by change, faced daily with new threats to its safety, the only way to conserve is by innovating. The only stability possible is stability in motion.[4] According to Giamatti, "We do best when we remember institutions change so they may endure with a sense of their purpose and dignity, which sense is what differentiates endurance from mere survival."[5]

The only way to preserve values over time is to be involved continuously in renewal and change, thus finding ever fresh expressions for those values. When any organization decides it will seek to save its life by building walls against change, that organization is destined to lose its life and its vitality. It is through such concepts as "continuity and change" and "stability in motion" that we may find the path that leads to ever new organizational life.

Ongoing visioning becomes the means for this renewal. If a compelling vision is not present, or if the organization is not seeking a vision, then a vacuum is created. The result will be either no vision, or more likely, the presence of many small competing visions. In either case, the result is decline.

WHAT IS A VISION?

What is a vision? It is a dream. It is a picture of what is possible. Perhaps the best way to think of it is "a picture of a preferred future." Rosabeth Moss Kanter believes that such a picture must be in place before people can let go of the past and permit change to take place.[6] As Aristotle put it, "The soul . . . never thinks without a picture."

In a recent speech, Bishop Rueben P. Job defines and describes a vision in this way: "Vision is a gift from God. It is the reward of disciplined, faithful, and patient listening to God. Vision allows us to see beyond the visible, beyond the barriers and obstacles to our mission. Vision 'catches us up,' captivates and compels us to act. Vision is the gift of eyes of faith to see the invisible, to know the unknowable, to think the unthinkable, to experience the not yet. Vision allows us to see signs of the king-

dom now, in our midst. Vision gives us focus, energy, the willingness to risk. It is our vision that draws us forward."

The vision represents the story through which one sees reality.
It gives meaning, direction, and life to one's efforts. For example,
a pastor and congregation develop together a bold vision of what
it means for that church to minister faithfully in the present,
while they also do those things essential for the church to be
strong in ten years. The vision comes to give direction to the priorities and efforts of the pastor and the people of the congregation. Now, anyone looking at that church would see activities by
pastor and people that seem common and ordinary. However,
these daily tasks are not ordinary either to the people involved or
to their mission because they are a part of a great vision. The
vision becomes for them the story through which they see reality.
Thus, that which may look no different from what is happening
with other pastors and other congregations is very different.

What John W. Gardner says about a great civilization can be
said about strong and vital organizations: "A great civilization is a
drama lived in the minds of a people. It is a shared vision; it is
shared norms, expectations, and purposes."[7]

Importance of Vision

*The cities and mansions that people dream of are those in which they
finally live.*

Lewis Mumford

"The very essence of leadership," says the longtime president
of Notre Dame, Father Theodore Hesburgh, is that "you have to
have a vision. It's got to be a vision you articulate clearly and
forcefully on every occasion. You can't blow an uncertain trum-
pet."[8] Today's church leaders would also do well to heed
Drucker's call for leaders to develop a vision around which people can have a passion.[9]

Such passion for a vision is not only needed for the benefit of
the organization, but also for the benefit of the leader as a person. "The only true happiness," according to John Mason
Brown, "comes from squandering yourselves for a purpose."[10]
William Blake's dictum—"What is now proved was once only

imagin'd"—is absolutely true in the way organizations, including the church, move from the present to a preferred future. Visioning is the imagination that gives inspiration and direction.

"Vision permeates our thoughts, desires, interests, ideals, imagination, feelings, and body language; it is our world view, our sense of life, our basic orientation towards reality. Our vision gives rise to our character, to our style of life, to our tone of being in the world. Vision is the way we grasp the complexity of life; it involves the meaning and value that we attach to the complexity of life as a whole and to the things of life in particular." In these words John Navone makes his contention that the existence of vision is fundamental to human life.[11]

While president of Yale University, A. Bartlett Giamatti spoke about what was needed to address the serious problems and challenges facing higher education in the United States. Try reading what he said below by substituting "churches" for "higher education" and "church" for "campus":

> The most pressing need in higher education in the next ten years is not for management strategies. It is for debate on each campus, led by its leaders, as to what the purposes and goals of each campus are—for only in the open arrival at some shared consensus of what the contour, the shape, the tendency, of the campus or of higher education will be can the drift of American higher education be halted; can the further internal fragmentation of campuses be forestalled; can the rush to special interest be reversed; can the public's faith that these places know what they are about, know why they exist and where they are going, be restored.[12]

Characteristics of a Vision

1. A vision is related to mission but different.

A vision must be clearly related to and grow out of the mission of an organization, but it is also different.

The most severe limitation of most local church mission statements is that they are so generic it is hard to use them to know what to do next. They often are of little help in making choices among the good alternatives always before a church that seek a claim on time, energy, and resources.

One way to think about the distinction between a mission and a vision is to think of the mission as "what we exist to do" and a vision as "what God is calling us to do in the immediate future (next year, next three years, or some other time period)." The mission may be "to bear witness to Jesus Christ in our community and beyond," and the vision that emerges may be "to move from what people experience as a cold and impersonal church to a warm and caring church."

2. A vision is unique.

Mission statements also tend to be so general that they could be used for any number of churches.

A vision is different in that it is unique. It should fit only a particular church at a particular moment in history. It is that specific. A vision such as "We need to engage, get to know, and develop ministries with the immediate neighborhood of our church between Third Avenue and Jefferson Street" would be hard to apply to another church.

3. A vision focuses on the future.

A vision honors the past, indeed is made possible by the past, but focuses on a preferred future. The object of attention in a vision is on the future. The two previous vision illustrations not only reflect current problems (cold church, no neighborhood involvement), but also, and more importantly, hold out preferred futures (warm church, engaged church).

4. A vision is for others.

The focus of a vision is on outcomes, results, and contributions for others. A vision does not focus on some goal of success such as being the largest church in the community, but it addresses needs related to the mission in challenging ways. Any institutional successes emerge as a result of being faithful to the mission. The vision always relates to meeting needs. While the institutional needs of the churches should be served through our two vision illustrations, the primary concern of the visions is for people who are currently not being served by the churches.

5. A vision is realistic.

A vision should be realistic because it is rooted in the people who make up the organization and in the reality of the current historical situation. If a group develops a vision well (in the midst of the people and facts), then the vision will be realistic. A vision needs to be sufficiently realistic for there to be some reasonable hope of success. Otherwise visions become fanciful imaginings or pipe dreams. These serve the interests of no one. No matter how compelling is the need for evangelism, a vision "to double our membership in one year" is unrealistic for nearly all churches.

6. A vision is lofty.

Equally important is the need for the vision to be lofty and inspiring. It should set a high standard and a target not easily attainable. The vision should be values-filled and show that the group has made a choice among values. Visions finally become questions of values. Visions come from the heart and represent our strongest values and commitments.

Remember that visions represent dreams about preferred futures. One way to discover a sense of your own vision and the values that undergird it is to complete the statement made famous by Martin Luther King, Jr., "I have a dream that. . . ." How would you complete that sentence for your church? How would others in your church complete the sentence? The answers are the beginning of a vision.

7. A vision is inviting.

A vision should be an attractive, clear, compelling, and appealing picture of what the future can be. Vision is a "see" word; it is a picture of a preferred future. It should be inviting and should claim the minds and hearts of persons in the organization. Passive and ho-hum visions will not inspire people.

The famous football coach Vince Lombardi said that the best coaches always know what the end result of a play looks like. Even if you have never seen the play run perfectly, you never lose the picture. "If you don't know what the end result is supposed to look like," he said, "you can't get there."[13] It is such a picture toward which good coaches coach. So it is that a vision provides a picture toward which leaders and groups move together.

In our illustrations, the prospect of a warm and caring church or a community-involved church should represent a desirable future for current church members, even those who may be part of the problem in the current situation.

8. A vision is a group vision.

An effective vision is a vision shared by members of the group. A vision is not a collection of individual visions with the leader simply collecting ideas and putting them together; nor is it an imposed vision in which the leader comes with her or his own dream and seeks to make it become a reality. The vision needs to "ring true" for most of the people.

The vision of a warm and caring church will not motivate anyone if there is not a broad realization of the need for such change.

9. A vision is good news and bad news.

A vision holds in it both promise and judgment. It is the promise of a better future. However, within the promise is some degree of judgment of the past and present. This means that what is received as good news by some will be received as bad news by others. The vision of a neighborhood-involved church may reflect judgment on years of clergy and lay leadership.

The title of a book by William K. McElvaney, *Good News Is Bad News Is Good News* (Orbis Books, 1980), presents the dilemma very well. Good news comes to us first as bad news because it represents judgment and the need for change. If the response is one of faithfulness, then what appears to be bad news becomes true good news for us. It comes to be the only way we can live because it does reflect what God intends for us now and in the future.

We are called to help ourselves and others remember that the reign of God is not yet. The incompleteness of our times always calls for recognizing limitations and moving toward that preferred future to which God is calling us. Although there is always some degree of judgment of the past, a good vision is so rooted in mission and history that persons who genuinely care will come to identify with the new vision.

10. A vision is a sign of hope.

A vision should inspire hope. A vision says in a dramatic way what is possible if people work together. It is a way of saying, "Look at what is possible for us!" It represents a belief that people can make the difference.

To this extent it is a great sign of hope. When there is no

hope within an organization, there is despair and a lack of motivation and energy to accomplish the mission.

To help create and identify with a compelling shared vision is one way the leader expresses hope in the future of the organization. If a leader genuinely has no hope for the future of the organization, there can be no motivation for that leadership. In that case, the leader should leave. Without hope there can be no vision and no leadership. Pastors who have reached a point of despair about the future in their present assignments need, for their sakes and for the sake of their church members, to find a way out of that situation as soon as possible.

SOURCES FOR VISIONING

During my first year as president of Saint Paul School of Theology, the question people most often asked was, "What is your vision for Saint Paul?" I feel sure that my answer did not give people either encouragement or confidence. I always replied, "I don't have one." I probably could have worded my reply a bit more helpfully. It did, however, reflect my feeling that a vision is not something one can bring into institutional leadership as a president, or into local church leadership as a pastor. We all bring to any leadership position important values and ideas. In my case, I had commitments and convictions about the church, theological education, and the practice of ministry. However, that is very different from coming into a leadership position with an exact picture of what you want the seminary to be, and then using your position and efforts to make the seminary a replica of your image.

We do not develop visions apart from the setting of leadership and then bring them in. They emerge, though not automatically and not without great effort and creativity. Visions cannot be imposed. They will not be accepted if they do not make sense and fit. It is not so much a matter of ownership of the vision by the group, as important as that is. It is an issue of a vision being the appropriate vision for particular people in a particular organization with a particular mission at a particular moment in history. "A flawed and inadequate vision," Denham Grierson writes, "can be as damaging as no vision at all."[14]

A. Identity and Vocation

The first source for visioning is identity and vocation. An important question we need always to ask is, "For what are we here?" Before a vision can emerge, an organization must be clear about its mission, its calling.

Clearly the church needs renewal. That renewal will not come from imitating the past, or in reacting to what we do not like, or in copying other social or political models. Renewal will come, as it always does, in a rediscovery of identity and vocation.

David Roozen says that mainline churches have "lost their internal sense of identity." Another observer points out that "not only are the traditional denominations failing to get their message across, they are increasingly unsure just what that message is."[15]

Vocation is perhaps the best word to use to describe what we normally talk about as the mission or purpose of an organization. What is the calling of the organization?

The vocation or calling is captured in the congregation's identity. Grayson L. Tucker has identified from many influential writers the following observations regarding the identity of a congregation:

1. The identity of a congregation may be understood as a complex set of beliefs and values deeply held by its members. These convictions define the congregation's view of itself; they are potent beliefs and values that result from the congregation's history of relating to its external environment while maintaining its own inner life. This identity consists of a deep structure of meaning that is frequently beyond the members' capacity to articulate clearly.
2. The identity of a congregation is frequently revealed as one seeks to change it. The change effort gives rise to resistance that reveals underlying identity elements. (These first two principles suggest that a change in congregational identity occurs more readily when that change is less threatening.)
3. The identity of a congregation has a vital connection with its own history. In changing a congregation's identity, it is crucial to take this history into account and to uncover the connections between the congregation's past and its new future.
4. The identity of a congregation, like that of an individual, is closely tied to its sense of mission; a change of identity is almost synonymous with being captured by a new sense of mission.
5. The identity of a congregation, like an individual's, must be approved by significant others. What we see in ourselves needs to be congruent with what significant others see in us.

6. A healthy congregational identity will be marked by flexibility and openness to change.

7. A healthy congregational identity cannot be considered a permanent possession; it is constantly lost and regained.

8. The identity of a congregation will include both positive and negative elements. Even when things look most bleak, there is an underlying, healthy core upon which any movement toward change can build.

9. Congregational health is strengthened when positive identity beliefs and values are broadly held and prized by the large majority of its members.

10. Congregational identity is determined by the convictions of that congregation's significant leaders, especially the pastor; this formation process is heavily influenced by worship and preaching.[16]

Developing an Identity Statement can be a useful way to get at the issue of vocation. An Identity Statement consists of two components: mission and values.

The mission statement should be one simple sentence that states clearly and succinctly what the organization exists to do. The mission represents an organization's reason for being.

The values section will be longer and will describe the commitments of the organization that shape the way the organization does its work. If the mission states what the organization exists to do, values describe how it will be done. In some ways the values represent the commitments, guidelines, and boundaries within which the organization will function to accomplish the mission.

Together mission and values form organizational identity. "Great leaders have always been able to discover core values and create an inspiriting, congruent reason for being," according to Art McNeil. "The organization's core values and reason for being," he continues, "must be meaningful at the emotional level; they've got to tug at the heartstrings and make people want to belong."[17]

Focusing on vocation helps groups go back to the source of their existence. Why are we here? Why were we created? What is God calling us to do? What is *the* story with which we identify and which gives us meaning?

Discussing such fundamental issues is crucial to clarify a commonly held understanding of identity. It forces people to go back to the original sources of text and history.

It is important to remember that developing an Identity Statement is not an end in itself. The Identity Statement needs to be realistic and vital so that it contributes to the visioning process. If it is simply pious and generic, then it will not be helpful. Mission and values need to match in a way that persons familiar with the organization will recognize the statement! Having broad involvement in the development of the Identity Statement will help this happen. A couple of exercises may be useful to identify values. To describe current reality people might be asked, "When you think of our church, what are the first words, images, or phrases that come to mind?" To discover the deepest hopes and dreams one might ask, "If a visitor came to your church next Sunday and asked several church members about the church, what would you hope they would say?"

A well-developed Identity Statement, which states clearly the mission and values of the organization, becomes the first source for visioning.

B. History

Vision will always grow out of the history of the organization or congregation. William Faulkner, through his character Gavin Stevens in *Intruder in the Dust,* reminds us that "The past is never dead. It's not even past." These are true words indeed when it comes to the life of a local church.

There is increasing attention to the importance of history for organizations. The history of an organization shapes to a great extent where it is, why it is there, and what the options are for the future. History should not determine vision, but if history is ignored, then the vision is likely to be inadequate.

A helpful way for a group to appropriate their history in a way that can inform and shape visioning is to do a history time line. There are many ways to do this. One way is simply to draw a long horizontal line with the year the church began on one end and the current year on the other. Then ask people in the group to put a mark on the time line to show when they entered the life of the church and describe what was happening at that time. During the discussion, others who entered the church around that time may participate. Then others in the group who entered before or after will describe another period of time. As they write important words from their descriptions on the time line, they can also write above and below the time line other important information to match the historical periods they are describing. Such information might include who the pastors were. Another strand running across might be important events happening in the nation at that time. They may even describe the time before the birth of present members because there will be people there who will know of the history through parents and grandparents, or by studying the history of the church. As a group works on the time line, distinct chapters in the church's history will emerge. Also everyone will begin to understand in a deeper way how the church came to be where it is today and what the positive and negative implications are for moving into the future.

C. Data gathering

For visioning to be effective, data gathering needs to take place both internally and externally. We need statistics and information about the internal life of the organization and about the external world in which the organization functions.

The first question to ask is, What do we need to know? The key here is not to think of all the categories of information that would be of interest, but to think of those things that are important for plans for the future. The second question is, How do we get this information?

For the local church, some data to gather may include:

- CHURCH MEMBERSHIP
- WORSHIP ATTENDANCE
- CHURCH SCHOOL MEMBERSHIP
- CHURCH SCHOOL ATTENDANCE
- BUDGET GROWTH
- ACTUAL RECEIPTS
- PERCENTAGE OF MEMBERSHIP CONTRIBUTING
- AGE MAKEUP OF MEMBERSHIP
- AGE MAKEUP OF CHURCH SCHOOL

- SOURCES OF NEW MEMBERS
- SOURCES OF MEMBERSHIP LOSS
- BREAKDOWN OF EXPENSE CATEGORIES OF BUDGET
- PARKING PLACES AVAILABLE, SPACE UTILIZATION
- STAFFING SIZE
- PARTICIPATION LEVELS IN VARIOUS MINISTRIES (E.G., MUSIC, CHILDREN'S, YOUTH, AND SO ON)
- GENDER AND RACIAL/ETHNIC COMPOSITION OF MEMBER-SHIP
- GENDER, RACIAL/ETHNIC, AND AGE COMPOSITION OF GOVERNING BOARD AND COMMITTEES

In terms of the external environment, some information to seek may be:

- LOCAL POPULATION FIGURES
- RACIAL/ETHNIC POPULATION FIGURES
- AGE MAKEUP OF POPULATION
- ECONOMIC STATISTICS
- DENOMINATIONAL AND JUDICATORY MEMBER-SHIP AND ATTENDANCE STATISTICS
- TRAFFIC PATTERN STATISTICS

Usually you will be seeking information for the past five to ten years. This makes it possible for you to see changes and trends. What you are looking for are clues, hints, hunches, and insights about the future and about planning for the future.

Many people need to be involved in this process. Different eyes will spot different things. It will be very important to look for what discoveries tend to be made repeatedly by different people and groups looking at the same material.

Many find it helpful to collect the various tables and statistics in a Baseline Data Book. The leader then asks many individuals and small groups to report the most important clues and insights for planning for the future. The important thing here is that people are working with the same trusted information.

It is amazing how people so often make decisions and plan for the future out of faulty assumptions and mythology. This will often come out in statements such as, "When Pastor Smith was here. . . ," or "We used to have more children than we could handle. . . ," or "We need more space. . . ." Trusted baseline data will help in seeing which assumptions are based on fact and which are not. It may be that we have as many children in church now as we have had for twenty years, or that we have plenty of square feet; but the issue is utilization or accessibility or renovating a section to make it usable, not building another building.

D. Environmental scanning

In environmental scanning the goal is to do a careful reading of both the internal and external environments of the organization. Groups need both dimensions for visioning, but normally give inadequate attention to the external environment. The focus is so inward that congregations scarcely look at what is happening all around the church. An ever-changing external environment requires more serious attention. Robert C. Worley speaks about the lack of clarity people generally have about the relationship between the environment and the behavior of an organization. In a stable environment, where the dominant religious, economic, political, and educational organization did not change rapidly, churches and other organizations could adapt slowly and without the obvious appearance of change. It was even possible in such a setting to assume that the church was independent or autonomous in relation to environmental fluctuations. Yet, he continues, most congregations are open systems. They experience the environment without protective shields. While congregations attempt to construct protective insulators, over time few are successful. The only safe beginning assumption today is that the church is in a dynamic relation to its environment.[18]

What one is looking for here includes opinions, perceptions, and ideas, as well as feedback regarding the current situation and future needs. Conversations, surveys, and small group discussions such as focus groups are some means often used to get at this source for visioning.

There is the need to get good feedback regarding specific areas (e.g., worship, education), and particular components of each (e.g., which components of the worship service are most meaningful, how do people evaluate different educational opportunities). There is also need for open-ended questions, such as: "What is one thing about our church that you hope never changes? If you could wave a magic wand and change one thing about our church, what would you change? What do you find most meaningful about our church? What do you find least meaningful about our church?"

As with data gathering, what one is looking for is clues for the future. Some clues might be discovered as answers to these questions suggested by Burt Nanus:

- Which individuals and institutions have a stake in the future of this organization, and what are they trying to make happen?
- What could happen if we continue on our present path without any changes?
- What early warning signals might we detect if the external environment were to change substantially?
- What future events could happen, both inside and outside our organization, that would have a big impact on us, and how likely are they to occur?
- How much leverage do we have to influence the course of events, and how could that leverage be applied?
- What options could be available to us, and what might their consequences be?
- What future resources might be available, and what would we have to do to secure them?
- Of the alternative futures that might occur for our organization and its environments, which are more likely to be favorable to our survival and success? [19]

Also important to consider for both the internal and external environment is what organizational consultant H. Rhea Gray calls "soft expert opinion." That means the best wisdom available about what is likely to happen within churches and communities in the immediate future, along with the monitoring of trends. The most valuable information to support farsightedness appears in trends; that is, patterns of movement of data over time that, if continued, suggest potential opportunities, vulnerabilities, or threats for the organization. [20]

E. Ministry by Wandering Around (M.B.W.A.)

Tom Peters has popularized M.B.W.A. in recent years to refer to "Management by Wandering Around." It describes the importance of the leader simply being present, and highlights how much can be learned merely by being involved with the people doing the work.

There are many possibilities for leadership in Ministry by Wandering Around, and it can become a vast resource for visioning. Pastors can conscientiously plan to do things that will make M.B.W.A. much more likely, and become adept at using the vast number of opportunities a pastor already has every day to practice M.B.W.A.

Visiting Sunday school classes, individual visits and conversations, just showing up at particular gatherings and activities—all offer opportunities for M.B.W.A. One large membership church staff reviews together several pages from their church pictorial directory every week at the staff meeting to see if there is anyone that no one of them knows. If that is the case, they decide together who will learn more about those persons and how. Any pastor can look at a few names from the membership each week and see if there is anyone that he or she has not gotten to know, or if there is someone there with whom there has not been any significant contact for a time.

Equally important is learning how to use opportunities that one already has through ongoing pastoral activities. For example, a pastor making a routine hospital visit to a longtime congregational member might say, "Mary, you have been a member of this church for forty years. What changes have you seen through those years?" or "What has been most important to you about the church through the years?" The next hospital visit might be with a new member of the church. That conversation might include: "Jim, you only began attending our church a couple of months ago. What was your first impression when you came?" Or, "You and your family have been in many churches with all your moves. How is our church like or different from the other churches in which you have been?"

Through such opportunities, another resource for visioning develops.

ROLE OF THE LEADER IN VISIONING

The first duty of a leader is to lead in the establishment of an appropriate and shared vision. This is one responsibility that cannot be delegated. While many other people will be involved, effective leaders accept their special responsibility for visioning.

Recognizing the absolute necessity for the formation of a compelling vision is the first role of a leader in the visioning process. Greenleaf asks the question, "Can a key leader accept that optimal performance rests, among other things, on the existence of a powerful shared vision that evolves through wide participation to which the key leader contributes, but which the use of authority cannot shape?"[21] He goes on to say that "an indispensable condition for the persuasive power [of leaders] to be effective is that the institution is living out a great dream. . . . Institutions function better when the idea, the dream, is to the fore."

A major study of leaders found that the spark of genius in the leadership function lies in this "transcending ability, a kind of magic, to assemble—out of all the variety of images, signals, forecasts and alternatives—a clearly articulated vision of the future that is at once simple, easily understood, clearly desirable, and energizing." All of the leaders seemed to have been masters at selecting, synthesizing, and articulating an appropriate vision of the future.[22]

Mary Parker Follett's description of the successful leader as one who "sees another picture not yet actualized" is about visioning. "[The leader] sees the things which belong in [her or his] present picture, but which are not yet there," she says. "Above all [the leader] should make [one's] coworkers see that it is not [the leader's] purpose which is to be achieved, but a common purpose, born of the desires and the activities of the group."[23]

Worley, in his study of congregational life, emphasizes the importance both of vision and the leader's role in establishing the vision. An important characteristic of leaders is the commitment to enable the congregation to generate a vision for itself that is helpful to its members and the community. "Leaders cannot impose a vision. They can initiate the processes and participate actively to contribute to the vision. They can also offer criteria by which the congregation can make discerning judgments about the quality of its vision. Congregations languish for lack of a worthwhile vision." His words—initiate, participate, and offer criteria—are very important dimensions of the unique role that leaders play in shaping a vision.

Worley helps us understand that leaders are more than "country club managers" who simply collect the ideas of the members of the group. "Leaders are generators of vision among God's people," he says, "and they hold certain criteria as a mirror before God's people to enable them to make judgments about the quality and adequacy of their vision."[24] Max DePree says that the first duty of the leader is to define reality.[25] The leader must continually do this in the visioning process through keeping people focused on identity and mission, and on the reality of the situation in which they are seeking to be faithful to God's call to ministry.

Pastors give time, energy, and passion to what they consider important. Hebrew Bible scholar Renita Weems-Espinoza spoke about pastors' reluctance to give teaching leadership regarding biblical scholarship; but her words can be applied to the task of leadership and visioning. She says to hesitant pastors, "Do you mean to tell me that you can convince your church to build a parsonage when they did not want to or carpet the sanctuary when they saw no need, and you are reluctant to suggest that Moses did not write certain books of the Bible or that there may be more than one Isaiah?" Pastors who would be leaders need to understand that vigorous engagement in visioning is at the heart of their role.

Process of Visioning

There is no freeway to the future. No paved highway from here to tomorrow. There is only wilderness. Only uncertain terrain. There are no road maps. No signposts. So pioneering leaders rely upon a compass and a dream.

James M. Kouzes and Barry Z. Posner, *The Leadership Challenge*

The process of visioning is neither simple nor easy. It takes a long time to shape, and when it emerges, it does not come forth fully formed. Furthermore, it takes even longer to be able to put the vision into words that adequately capture the vision that is emerging.

Kouzes and Posner have compared this process to preparing for an expedition. When one begins, there may only be a vague desire to go somewhere. After months of planning, the details about the particular expedition become specific. In between, there are countless stages that help one move from the general to the specific, which is always the direction of visioning.[26]

A United Methodist bishop once said to me, "One of the most important things I do is to select district superintendents. What can I do other than pick good people that will fulfill this function better?" Out of that conversation came a plan: The bishop normally selects district superintendents in winter or early spring. The bishop would ask the new district superintendent to bring to annual conference in May a vision for the superintendent's ministry in this new position over the coming years. The bishop would then ask the new superintendent to spend the summer in conversations with all of the pastors of the district and with laypeople in all the churches. The superintendent would bring to the first cabinet meeting after Labor Day another one-sentence statement of vision for the superintendent's ministry. After the district superintendent conducted all the charge conferences in the fall, another vision statement would be requested around Christmastime. Then, finally, after the new superintendent had gone through the first round of appointment making in the spring, the bishop would ask for yet another vision statement at the end of the superintendent's first year of service. The bishop would then spend time with the superintendent talking about the vision, how the superintendent arrived at that vision, and how the bishop can be of help to the superintendent in achieving the vision.

In such a plan, it is very likely that the vision statements would change over the course of the year in which the superintendent prepared them. The movement in visioning is normally from general to specific. Early visions may appear on the surface more bold and visionary than later visions; but it is only through engagement with the specific situation that one comes to realize what is both bold and realistic within that context. General visions tend to be based on an inadequate understanding of the situation. Truly bold visions fit the reality of the situation. An outside observer may say about the superintendent's final vision, "Is that all you hope to accomplish?" The new superintendent may reply, "This may not be a bold vision in your situation but, believe me, this is a very bold vision given the reality of the situation I face."

Vision occurs not from flights of inspiration, according to Harvard Business School professor John P. Kotter, but "when a powerful mind, working long and hard on massive amounts of information, is able to see (or recognize in suggestions from others) interesting patterns and new possibilities."[27] This is what one is always looking for in the sources of visioning. The process is to take information that is already there (or can be obtained) and to work and live with it until the insights for visioning emerge.

Extraordinary visions come from ordinary sources. The sources represent simply what you, others, and the organization bring. Visions are rarely original. It is not so much inspiration, as it is paying attention to the situation and particularly to people. Listening is essential, especially hearing what is not being said. It is a matter of recognizing from all the information, feelings, and images the most appropriate symbols and images of the future. To do this one must become absorbed in the sources of visioning. One is constantly gathering, assessing, and using this information.

The leader may not talk explicitly about visioning. The process is far too subtle for that. If the process becomes too structured and formalized, it may lose its life. Specific time lines and votes generally are irrelevant. Wide participation in the visioning process (because it must be a *shared* vision) is essential, and the approach to this participation cannot be simplistic or mechanical. The important result is for the vision to ring true to the people and find affirmation within the group, not just for the leader to be able to show that there were many votes or that every group or person was involved in every step. The reality of involvement is more important than the formal process. It is far more important in the end for people to feel they were involved, by seeing themselves represented in the results and the vision, than for the leader to have a process that tries to have everyone involved in everything.

While wide participation in the visioning process is essential, the leader has a very special role. Quite often the leader is the only one in touch with the many dimensions of the visioning process. The leader thus has a role not only to keep that process going, but also to recognize clues to the vision. It is essential that the leader recognize this creative role rather than view the visioning process as simply something to facilitate. The leader is searching for a vision. Finally, it must be a vision that is articulated, tested, and refined. In all likelihood, no one else in the organization is either giving, or having the opportunity to give, the kind of time and intensity to visioning that the leader is giving.

All the knowledge and experience gained from the process of visioning represent merely resources, and these are not enough by themselves to form a vision. Visions do not leap forth fully formed. The data must be extracted, refined, and processed. One must be able to see what no one else has seen before. One must be able to hear what has not been heard before. It is almost as if one is being asked to see what cannot be seen, and hear what is not being said.

Remember, this is not just a matter of giving people what they want. People are not able to speak for the future very well. The *Saturday Evening Post* went out of business giving people what they said they wanted.[28] The task of editorial leadership is not simply to give people what they want today, but to be so in touch with a reading constituency that one is able to stay one step ahead. It is to give them what they want and need, though it is so new that they do not yet articulate it for themselves.

Leadership is the ability to anticipate the future based on the past and present. Someone has said, "Our leaders tell us what we are thinking. Our leaders tell us what we are feeling." When visions that are true emerge, the response of the people in the group is a nod of recognition, identification, and affirmation.

Callahan says that the missionary pastor—his model for the pastoral leadership needed in local churches today—must have a sense of vision that draws on powerful imagination, unusual discernment, and foresight. This vision will be responsible and realistic, not naive and idealistic; courageous and compassionate, not timid and calculating; prayerful and powerful, not self-centered and weak.[29]

Role of Intuition and Discernment in Visioning

If [the vision] seems to tarry, wait for it; it will surely come, it will not delay.

Habakkuk 2:3*b* NRSV

Intuition and discernment are the wellsprings of vision. In visioning, one's prayer must always be that of the writer of Ephesians: "I pray that the God of our Lord Jesus Christ . . . may give you the spiritual powers of wisdom and vision" (1:17 NEB).

Visioning is more relational and holistic than ordered and sequential. It is more intuitive than intellectual. It is more spiritual than scientific. In this sense, visioning is very much like other creative processes.[30]

Grierson suggests that what we need is that which Heidegger calls meditative thinking. Meditative thinking is a style of thinking that is synthetic, imaginative, holistic, and metaphorical. Meditative thinking seeks by imagination and intuition to grasp the webs of significance that hold the meanings of the people.

This does not suggest an antirational mode of inquiry; it is not an invitation to lapse into romanticism about the life of the congregation. "It is to suggest rather that if one seeks the subtle and elusive webs of meaning that bind together the inner life of a community," Grierson says, "they will not be captured in the net of analytic thought."

C. S. Lewis makes the distinction in this way: "I am a rationalist. For me reason is the natural organ of truth; but imagination is the organ of meaning." Meaning, therefore, comes from the "integration of both reason and imagination in which reason is guided not by its own structural logic but that which comes cooperatively from the domain of imagination."[31]

For the pastor the closest thing to a visioning process is probably the preparation of a sermon. There are things that the preacher can do that will make a good sermon more likely. Selecting a text early, studying many and different readings of the text over a period of time, studying the key words, reviewing commentaries, praying and meditating on the scripture—all represent steps a preacher must take in preparing a sermon. Yet, as every preacher knows, simply going through certain steps will not guarantee that the sermon on Sunday will come alive and be a moment in which God is able to use the preacher to speak a distinctive word of salvation for the people.

The leader requires discernment to distinguish between what is actually healthy and what merely appears to be living. The wise leader is able to discern the difference between the living edges and the dying ones within an organization,[32] while these may both seem to have the same importance or insignificance to the casual observer or to the leader without discernment.

Good leaders have what Bennis calls the "Gretzky Factor." Wayne Gretzky, the best hockey player of his generation, said it is not as important to know where the puck is now as it is to skate to where the puck is going to be. Leaders have that sense of where the organization is going and where the organization must be if it is to grow and thrive.[33]

The movement in visioning is from simplicity to complexity back to simplicity. A pastor goes to a new church with a simple sense of vision based on what the pastor knows by reputation or limited knowledge about the church. Most of us have impressions about churches even when we know very little about them. However, once the pastor arrives and begins to work, what seemed very clear-cut and simple a few months before now is complex. The history, values, problems, and opportunities all are much more complex than they were before the pastor became immersed in the life of the congregation. The pastor now may think it is unlikely that one clear vision will emerge when there are dozens of urgent matters crying to be priorities.

Yet, if the pastor and people stay with the visioning process, there should come a point when the maze of data, feelings, and impressions that made for such complexity now begins to give forth a clear insight, which can be the beginning of a simple and powerful vision for the future. Out of the many things that are needful, the one thing that will show the way to the future emerges in simple terms.

The vision that emerges may appear to outsiders very much like the original vision; both are simple. However, there is a world of difference between the two. The original vision reflected a simplicity based on lack of knowledge, experience, and involvement. The simplicity of the new vision grows out of deep wisdom drawn from much data gathering and soul-searching, hundreds of conversations and hours of reflection. The original vision has little, if any, power. The emerging vision has the power of truth behind it because it reflects what this church is, what it must do, and where it must go to be God's faithful instrument for redemption in the world.

"I would not give a fig for the simplicity this side of complexity," Justice Oliver Wendell Holmes is reported to have said, "but I would give my life for the simplicity on the other side of complexity." Also remember the caution given by Alfred North Whitehead, "Seek simplicity and then distrust it."[34] Visioning is a continuing process of discernment.

Effective leaders come to have a sense of where the whole organization is going and must go. One important contribution of the leader to the visioning process is selecting, synthesizing, and articulating themes and ideas that emerge. This serves the purposes of both accountability and furthering the visioning process. Having to articulate what one is beginning to think and feel requires a kind of vulnerability, but it does create an important accountability mechanism. A leader cannot develop a vision for others to live by.

We also need to remember how very much our own values influence visioning. Two leaders may be exposed to the very same knowledge and experience in the sources of visioning, and yet be led to very different visions because of different values and different views of reality. This is something a leader should celebrate because it means that everything that one brings to leadership as a person does contribute. The process truly is creative and spiritual and not mechanistic, so different persons doing the visioning would be unlikely to come to the same conclusions. The leader also must be open to God's wisdom working through other minds and value systems to test the organization's vision. Such testing is to make sure that the vision is not a mere extension of the leader's personal values without respect for the mission of the institution and the history, values, and needs of the people.

FUNCTIONS OF A VISION

1. A vision unites.

What unites a group is the idea represented in the vision, not a charismatic leader or shared loyalty to the organization. The vision presents a common interpretation of reality and of the future. The persuasion that is needed to move a group to action then becomes the persuasive power of the vision. Is it true? Is it worthy? If so, it will bear with it the power needed to bring people together and move them forward together.

Leadership is always about corporate purpose and group effort. To achieve corporate purpose a group must have a basic object to which they look as a guide for the future. Worley says that a hopeful vision for the whole congregation brings at-oneness to congregational life and serves to guide, direct, and judge human efforts toward that end.[35]

2. A vision energizes.

When there is a powerful and compelling vision, people look to the future with hope. Such a vision can lift people out of their ordinary and conventional ways of thinking and working. It gives a boost to morale and a lift to spirits.

A vision helps people understand that their efforts are a part of something larger than themselves. A vision shows how their individual labors contribute to something more important than the sum of those efforts. People come to think of themselves as more important and their participation in the organization as something significant in their lives, indeed as a source of pride.[36]

A worthy vision penetrates deeply into the psyches of all whom the vision draws. "The test of greatness in a dream," says Greenleaf, "is that it has the energy to lift people out of their moribund ways to a level of being and relating from which the future can be faced with more hope than most of us can summon today."[37]

3. A vision focuses priorities.

A vision helps keep priorities in order. Intensity coupled with commitment is powerful. Strength is always found in focus. No organization, no matter how strong in terms of history, people, and resources, will be strong if it squanders those resources in multiple directions without a clear focus. A vision keeps people focused on what they together have agreed they are about.

A congregation can make every policy and decision with reference to the vision. In essence people are always asking, "What does the vision require of us?" If the vision is true, lively, and working within the group, the question may not be asked directly, but it will serve to guide those decisions.

Someone has said that a vision serves as a lens through which we are able to see the future more clearly. The future is something of a blur until the vision serves to focus the lens. It is much as one might focus the lens of a projector until what has been a blur becomes perfectly clear. Once there is clarity about where the group is going, then they find it easier to set priorities and make decisions.

Focusing priorities is always an important challenge before a church. Churches rarely face good options versus bad options. The decisions tend to revolve around the competing claims of good causes. However, given limited time, energy, and resources, they must always make judgments. If there is no focus, there will be little to show for efforts. Yet if there is a clear focus on the vision, then the group makes every decision in light of the vision. Questions that at first seem unrelated to the vision are asked in relation to the vision, because that is what is on everyone's mind. And the reason it is on everyone's mind is because everyone has become convinced that this is what God is calling them to in the immediate future.

The focus of the vision helps a group stay clear about direction and not get distracted about all the other projects and possibilities that are available. The true and compelling shared vision is a way for the organization to say for this moment in history: This is what we believe God is calling us to do. This is where we are going. Other activities are diversions.[38]

4. A vision serves as the ultimate standard.

Every person and constituency of the organization stands subordinate to the vision. Like all organizations, churches in their activities and efforts can easily become merely a collection of group interests. Over time different groups develop plans and make claims on the energy and resources of the church without measuring them against mission and vision. A vision represents that commitment, larger than any one individual or group, to which we all give our loyalty and commitment.

Rosabeth Moss Kanter has observed that no matter how true and compelling a vision is, it must be repeated over and over for it to stick as a guiding principle for everyone in the organization. There can never be too much redundancy. Leaders have a special role in repeating the group's shared vision in various ways. People hear so many things from a leader that repetition of the vision is essential for people truly to come to hear and believe it.[39]

One image that is useful in helping people think about the role of a vision as ultimate standard is an inverted pyramid.[40] In a traditional pyramid the point at the top can represent the way a traditional organizational structure works: a leader or leaders decide what is important and everyone below is to accomplish those goals. With an inverted pyramid, the largest part is at the top and represents the vision. Everyone is included below the vision. The key role of leaders in the group is to make sure that all efforts and energies within the pyramid are flowing toward the vision, and no persons or groups are pulling out of the pyramid to set up shop for themselves.

Whenever there is a move outside the pyramid (vision), whether it is the men's Bible class, music ministry, or even an important congregational value, leadership requires that the vision be lifted up as the "invisible leader." Therefore, the leader's questions will not focus so much on rights or power, but on the vision and how what is under discussion relates to and serves the vision.

James D. Whitehead and Evelyn Eaton Whitehead use the image of an orchestra. The leader must have the ability to focus the group's energies, to channel diverse resources into an organic whole. For the group to be effective, the leader must exercise control. But the leader's control exists in the musical score. Both the group and the leader are accountable to something beyond individual preference, the script that they all follow. Both the conductor and the musicians know the score. There is control present, but it is not manipulation. The common vision exercises the control required for the pursuit of a common goal, and does so in a context of mutual accountability.[41]

Does this mean that group interests get lost? No. While there is one overarching vision for the organization, there will be many different and subordinate visions present. The same visioning process that takes place for the church as a whole needs to take place within children's ministry, education, and within almost every area of the church's life. These subordinate visions, while consistent and compatible with the total vision, will be different. Some people will come to identify with one of the subordinate visions far more closely than they would ever be able to do with the larger vision. The subordinate visions are not competitors with the overall vision, but have been measured against the larger vision and represent a more specific expression of the vision. The vision needs to be open enough to provides a basic tune for the congregation, and to leave enough freedom for some persons to sing different verses of the same song.

5. A vision raises sights.

A vision sets a standard of high goals and expectations. It raises the level of what everyone expects of themselves and others. With the vision, far more will be expected and will be accomplished.

Setting high goals tends to bring out the best in people. Woodrow Wilson said once that the reason the faculty debates at Princeton were so intense was because the stakes were so low. That is the way it often works in local churches. Have you ever noticed how intense the differences over minor issues can become?

Without a compelling vision there will be a vacuum in which almost nothing is happening, but in which almost every problem becomes exaggerated. A pastor told me that in his church there were two groups of people, older members who had been in the church for years and a significant group of young couples with small children. The young people were not the children of the older persons, since their children had left years ago to find employment in other areas. These younger persons had moved in more recently. The pastor said every issue became a conflict between the younger and older members. At the time of our conversation the burning issue was the upset of the older persons having to pay for nursery care for the children of the younger people during church worship and other activities. The issue had become very politicized and had drawn everyone into the matter. This is an example of what happens when the energies of people are not being devoted to a great vision.

6. A vision invites and draws others.

A vision invites and draws others by the very force of its appeal. A vision is a picture of a preferred future. It paints a picture that is exciting and challenging to all who know about it. It brings with it energy and commitment. These things lead other people to want to join the effort.

Rosabeth Moss Kanter says that a vision is a direction, not a destination. It is a picture of what might be, but it is never so specific that it cannot change.[42] This makes it possible to invite people to join in the pilgrimage toward this preferred future, one that they will help shape by their involvement. People are challenged and drawn by dynamic directions far more so than by static destinations.

POSSIBLE PITFALLS

1. Visioning signifies dissatisfaction with what currently exists. It opens one to the criticism of not properly appreciating the past. The past is extremely important in visioning, but the primary focus of visioning is the future. The vision will build on the past and be an extension of the past, but it will be different. Leadership is about change, and leadership deals with the future.

2. A vision exposes the future that we want and opens the possibility of conflict with competing visions. When there is not a vision, there is either a vacuum or competing visions. When the visioning process begins you will come to realize that there are competing images about a preferred future present within the group. These are already present and are shaping decisions. The difference now is that the visioning process brings to light these competing images, and they will have to be examined and measured in the total group.

3. A vision forces us to hold ourselves accountable for acting in ways consistent with the vision. This is true for leaders and

true for the organization. Visions will not recruit anyone if they are not matched by life-style.[43]

4. The vision will require courage. The vision should not require that the leader act like a martyr, but there are risks involved. In her study of change, Rosabeth Moss Kanter points out that people she calls "change masters" are willing to take risks, but usually not big risks.[44] The risks may seem greater to outside observers than is the case because others are not in touch with the actual situation as the leader is.

Still, a degree of courage is often necessary. Unfortunately, people sometimes use courage as an excuse for aggression. Effective leaders use courage to face difficult circumstances within an organization and are attentive to how they do so:
—They are honest and straightforward. They help define the problem or issue clearly for people.
—They put themselves inside the circle of the problem.
—They reassure the people of their expectation that the issue will be resolved and of their commitment to work things out.

EXERCISES

1. Complete the following sentence, "For my church I have a dream that someday. . . ."

2. Read the "I Have a Dream" speech by Martin Luther King, Jr., and then ask what vision does this speech represent.

3. Read the following biblical passages and ask the question, "What dream is reflected in each passage?" How would the "I have a dream. . . ." sentence be completed based on these passages? Discuss with others.

> Genesis 2:4–3:7
> Exodus 3:1-14
> Exodus 16:1-30
> Amos 5:21-24
> Matthew 28:16-20
> Luke 1:46-55
> Luke 4:18-21

4. Write a mission statement for your church: one sentence that states what your church exists to do.

5. Make a list of the most important values of your church.

6. Write your vision for your church as you understand it today: one sentence that reflects what you feel God is calling your church to do now given your mission and values.

THREE

TEAM

God put all the separate parts into the body on purpose. If all the parts were the same, how could it be a body? As it is, the parts are many but the body is one. The eye cannot say to the hand, "I do not need you," nor can the head say to the feet, "I do not need you."

1 Corinthians 12:18-21 JB

Lots of people have the power to stop things.

Rosabeth Moss Kanter

Visions that only the leaders see are insufficient to create organized movement. Leaders must inspire others to see the exciting future possibilities of a new vision.[1] Leaders must be able to enlist many other people in the cause of the vision.

A vision cannot be established by edict. It is an act of persuasion. It is the creation of an enthusiastic and dedicated commitment to a vision because it is "right for the times, right for the organization, and right for the people who are working in it." Years ago Mary Parker Follett captured this spirit when she observed that successful leaders focus on a common purpose, born of the desires and needs of the people most involved.[2]

Leaders are called to build teams with spirit and cohesion, teams that feel like family.[3] While much of the conventional

69

wisdom about leadership seems to assume a leader working alone, the solo leader is rarely associated with effective leadership. Most effective leadership involves a number of people acting in a team relationship. It is much more a social process than people often assume.[4]

The more successful an organization is, the more it requires a team for effective leadership.[5] Thus, effective leaders understand the importance of the team and exert great effort in building the team. They understand what it means both to be a leader and a servant of the team, and they willingly and often acknowledge indebtedness and gratitude to the members of the team.

COMMUNITY

Team building is similar to the establishment and development of community within a congregation. "Community, in its simplest terms," according to Evelyn Eaton Whitehead and James D. Whitehead, "is a gathering of people who support one another's performance. . . . Community is the place where we learn how to hold one another."[6]

John W. Gardner contends that what we think of as a failure of leadership on the contemporary scene may be traceable to a breakdown in the sense of community. "Leaders are community builders," he maintains, "because they have to be." He suggests the following ingredients of community:

1. Wholeness incorporating diversity
2. A shared culture
3. Good internal communication
4. Caring, trust, and teamwork
5. Group maintenance and government
6. Participation and the sharing of leadership tasks
7. Development of young people
8. Links with the outside world

"Skill in the building and rebuilding of community is not just another of the innumerable requirements of contemporary leadership," concludes Gardner. "It is one of the highest and most essential skills a leader can command."[7]

WHO IS ON THE TEAM?

Key Leaders

Defining the team is crucial. The key question here is: Who are the people without whom the vision cannot be realized?

All paid staff generally should be a part of the team because they have a distinctive relationship to the church and the vision. Then there will be people on the team by virtue of a position they hold that relates to the particular nature of the vision. If persons hold those positions who are unable or unwilling to share in accomplishing the vision, then serious consideration has to be given to how changes can be made. It probably will be impossible, or at least unwise, to try to function around the position. It is equally dangerous to expect someone not committed to a vision to carry it out. Some may be on the team because of unusual influence and credibility within the church. Some may be on the team who are not a part of the local congregation, but their expertise, support, or cooperation will be crucial to the fulfillment of the vision.

This team will not be very large. Once established in the mind of the leader, these people are never far from the thinking of the leader. The leader is constantly searching for ways to stay in touch, involve, support, encourage, cultivate—in other words, build the team.

Leaders build strong teams. These teams have high motivation, energy, and commitment. The team knows you as leader, and knows your hopes and dreams. More important, they understand the vision of the church. They know the vision and values of both you and the church so well that they immediately can detect behavior that does not conform to the shared vision.

Stakeholders

In addition to the team there are many groups and constituencies that comprise a church. Some organizations refer to such groupings as stakeholders—those who have a stake in the well-being and future of the organization. Effective leadership requires the cooperation of most of the people involved in the organization, so attention to stakeholders becomes very important. As pastors we often think about meeting the needs of individuals. However, in addition to being a collection of individuals, the church is also composed of groups with like interests.

The key question here is: "What does each group have a right to expect from this church?" Notice that the question is not "What does each group want?" Since there are always limited resources and limited time, there is no way to meet all needs. However, a church should be providing what each group has a right to expect. These decisions require judgment, and a leader is making judgments all the time.

For example, here are some ways to think about what stakeholders expect: What does any shut-in member of this church have a right to expect from the church? What do parents of preschool children have a right to expect from this church? What does any youth in this church have a right to expect? What do parents whose children go through our Christian education program have a right to expect that their children will receive as a result of that experience? What does any member of this church have a right to expect regarding financial matters? One can continue to ask such questions about various groupings within the church and about various program areas. Some relatively simple work by thoughtful people will achieve a degree of consensus on these matters. Certainly enough consensus can be achieved to decide upon foundational expectations.

Work with stakeholders is as important as, even if different from, work with the key members of the team. Rosabeth Moss Kanter has pointed out that in organizations many people have the power to stop things. She notes that even groupings that, according to formal organizational charts, seem to be the most powerless have veto power in many ways. In the local church people often express this veto power by lack of involvement. Peter Drucker has turned his attention to management in not-for-profit organizations in recent years. While acknowledging that the differences between for-profit and not-for-profit organizations are not nearly so great as people tend to assume, he does say there are a few key differences. One of these differences is that in not-for-profit organizations, no one group can say "yes" by themselves, while there are many groups that can say "no."

In addition to internal stakeholders, the leader also needs to consider external stakeholders. Many external people, interests, and organizations have a stake in what happens in your church. One's local community and denomination come immediately to mind. However, there are usually other external stakeholders who need thought and concern. Today most organizations and their leaders are affected by decisions made outside their boundaries. All human systems (organizations, groups, communities) that make up the society and the world are increasingly interdependent. Nearly all leaders at every level carry on dealings with people and systems external to the one in which they themselves are involved. The greater the level of leadership, the greater the demands for such external relationships become.[8]

ROVING LEADERSHIP

Max DePree tells the following story:

It was Easter Sunday morning and the large church was filled. The processional was ready to begin. The three pastors, the senior choir, two children's choirs poised at the back of the church—weeks of planning and preparation were about to be fulfilled.

As the organist struck the first chord, a middle-aged man in the center of the church began to sweat profusely, turned an ashen gray, rose partially out of his seat, stopped breathing, and toppled over onto his daughter sitting next to him. And what did these pastors, organists, and choirs do? They did nothing.

But in less than three seconds, a young man with experience as a paramedic was at the stricken man's side. Quickly and expertly he opened the airway and restored breathing. After several minutes, making sure the sick man's condition was stabilized and on a signal from the paramedic, six men lifted him carefully and carried him quickly to the back of the church where he was laid on the floor to await the arrival of the ambulance, which, having been called for immediately by some unknown person, was already on its way.

When the man was laid on the floor near the waiting children's choir, two youngsters fainted. Two doctors from the congregation were immediately on the scene. One stepped in to help the young man care for the patient; the other immediately looked after the two children.

At this point a man thrust his head into the group gathered around the patient and said, "Are you going to want oxygen?" And when the doctor said, "Yes," he immediately handed it to him, having anticipated the need and gone to find the oxygen bottle.

While all these things were going on, the man's wife (who was in the senior choir and did not know what was happening—only that the service was being momentarily delayed) was sensitively informed and brought to her husband's side. Others quieted the children's choirs, reassured them that the man was going to be okay and that they should begin to compose themselves for the service. The paramedics arrived, put the man in the ambulance, and took him to the hospital.

As you can imagine, a tender and poignant service now began. At the end of the service, the pastor was able to announce that the man had suffered a severe allergic reaction; his condition was stable; the outlook was positive.[9]

Leadership is never fixed and static, but is fluid and dynamic. In this crisis the role of leader shifted among a paramedic, the doctor, several other laity, and the pastors. Not only is leadership spread throughout any organization, but the effective leader is one who is able constantly to shift roles among being leader, peer, and follower. The effective leader knows which role is appropriate under particular circumstances.

To illustrate what she called "multiple leadership," Mary Parker Follett tells a story of a new school teacher who apparently was not preparing the chalk boards and supplies at the end of the day as was customary in that school. The custodian had reminded her, but she had paid little, if any, attention. Finally, the custodian reminded her again of the procedure that teachers are to follow at the end of each day. When it became apparent that she did not see that as a part of her responsibilities, the custodian said, "Apparently, you have not worked under the supervision of a custodian before."[10] This was an area in which the custodian was the leader of the school. He had worked with the others in the school in developing an agreed-upon procedure. In this arena the teacher was the follower.

Every effective leader has those relationships in which he or she is either peer or follower. Leaders who must be the leader in every situation are rarely effective or respected. Good collegiality and good "followership" are just as important to effective leadership as good leadership. In some South Pacific cultures a speaker will hold a conch shell, symbolizing a temporary position of authority.[11]

DePree says that in organizations there are two kinds of leaders, hierarchical (positional may be a preferred designation) leaders and roving leaders. Positional leaders should seek to identify the roving leaders in order to support them and follow them, and should learn to exhibit the grace that enables the roving leader to lead.[12]

Roving leadership is possible when the vision is foremost in an organization. Since the vision is the "invisible leader" (a term used by Mary Parker Follett), then positional leaders are servants of that vision. Their concern is not who is doing the leading or who gets credit for success. The real fulfillment of the leader comes in the fulfillment and the realization of the vision, not in protecting one's status or position against infringement.

Positional leadership and roving leadership are not mutually exclusive. Each makes the other possible, and without both working together, genuine progress would not take place.

To summarize, roving leadership has two dimensions. There is the roving nature of leadership among the roles of leader, peer, and follower. There are also the complementary leadership roles of positional leadership and roving leadership, which arise from others within the group. A dynamic concept like roving leadership is helpful in that, despite talk of hierarchy, there is usually no "at the top" in an organization from the perspective of a leader. Almost no leader ever feels "at the top," but experiences leadership "in the middle," caught between competing groups, needs, and choices.

WAYS TO BUILD STRONG TEAMS

Effective leaders know how to put together effective teams. Team building may have some elusive qualities, but leadership studies have defined several steps:

1. Treat everyone with respect.

One way to build the team is to think of everyone with whom we work, including paid staff, as volunteers. The best people working as paid staff in an organization are like volunteers in that they probably could find good jobs many places, but choose to work in your organization. They stay not merely to get a paycheck or because they have no other options, but because they choose to stay. Volunteers do not need "contracts so much as they need covenants," and for them, relationships always count more than structure.[13]

Leaders do well to consider the Pygmalion effect.[14] In George Bernard Shaw's *Pygmalion,* Eliza Doolittle would always be a Cockney flower girl to Professor Henry Higgins. She knew that he could never accept the change in her, but would always see her as she used to be. As she told Freddy, "The difference between a lady and a flower girl is not how she behaves, but how she's treated. I shall always be a flower girl to Professor Higgins because he always treats me as a flower girl and always will; but I know I can be a lady to you because you always treat me as a lady and always will."

Most of us are aware of how important it is for followers to have faith in their leaders. Perhaps the more searching question to ask is whether "the leader believes in the followers."[15]

Regularly find ways to affirm to them that "you are our leader" in this particular area. Ask what they need from you for their leadership to be effective and fulfilling. Make sure they know that you look to them as leaders for specific dimensions of the mission, and that you regard them as valued and trusted colleagues in the leadership team.

2. Involve people.

A study of values and meaning in business organizations concluded that the answer to the question, "How should others be treated?" involves treating others with respect and involving people.[16] Involving as many people as possible in developing cooperative goals, planning, and problem solving will pay rich dividends.

A working principle of stewardship is that people give at their level of involvement. Team members and potential team members need ongoing opportunities for genuine and substantive involvement. A pastor discovered that the president of a major company was a church member and a regular worshiper. The pastor wanted this gifted leader on a key committee for the coming year; however, the nominations committee felt this person had not "worked his way up" to such an assignment. Frustrated, but not defeated, the pastor formed a special task group to help him as pastor think through some overall church issues; he included this business leader along with other potential leaders and church officers. In some ways this task group made the best use of the business leader's time and expertise. What may be more significant is that this gifted pastor found a way to involve a church member who had unusual promise for becoming a leader.

Another pastor served a church on the verge of a major building program just as a severe economic recession hit the city. The congregation had completed plans for the new building. The capital campaign for the project was to begin within six months. Should the campaign go ahead or be put on hold until the economy improved? Much of the church members' considerable wealth was secure and not subject to economic fluctuations; but the pastor knew that the uncertain economic conditions were making everyone more cautious. The faltering economy was on everyone's mind.

This thoughtful pastor asked, "Who are the persons without whom this financial campaign cannot succeed?" The list was small and remarkably easy for the pastor to compile. Some were on the building committee or finance committee, while others held no formal positions in the church. The pastor brought them together for a few sessions to serve as an informal group of advisers. He sought their help to determine how to think about his own leadership in this matter. They reviewed the history, discussed the building plans and the needs that led to them, and assessed the current dilemma. The pastor picked up no clear clues about the advisability of proceeding with the campaign until near the end of one session. A respected member of the group said, "I think we need to do this now, and I will commit $300,000." The others agreed and made their sizable commitments. Not only did the pastor get the answer he was seeking, but the congregation achieved most of the funding for the project through this process of involvement. If the group discussions had led to no enthusiasm from this group for an immediate campaign, then this information would have been just as valuable to the pastor.

The goal of such involvement is both to help people identify with the vision of the organization and, most importantly, to help them connect their own personal visions with the organization's vision. Not only does this lead to greater personal satisfaction, it also develops organizational strength and makes possible genuine leadership. As Mary Parker Follett says so well, "Whoever connects me with the hidden springs of life, whoever increases the sense of life in me, . . . is my leader."[17]

3. Foster collaboration.

Closely related to involving people is fostering collaboration. Collaboration acknowledges in a dramatic way our mutual need for and appreciation of one another. Here the leader constantly seeks to create interaction among the people involved so that they may find interactive and integrative solutions to problems and possibilities.

Basic change takes place very slowly, if at all, largely because "those with the power generally have no knowledge, and those with the knowledge have no power."[18] It is the task of the true leader to make sure that people who have the knowledge and people who can make change happen are working together.

Rather than seeing oneself as the hero who single-handedly resolves all problems, a wise leader brings together the right people and then asks the right questions. The leader encourages solutions to emerge from this genuine collaboration. Because of dilemmas that are hampering the church's mission, a pastor may bring together, for example, those responsible for the care of the physical facilities and those who lead youth ministry. Another may ask children's ministry leaders to collaborate with those responsible for music ministry.

A pastor of a fast-growing church realized there were two distinct opinions about how to handle the need for more parking and building space to accommodate the growth that all celebrated. Some felt they should purchase more property to add new parking and buildings. Others felt that good stewardship called for no physical expansion but rather the addition of multiple church schools and worship services. It was clear to the pastor that something had to be done and that either solution would be difficult and require the full support of the entire church.

This pastor brought together thoughtful and articulate representatives of both viewpoints, carefully including people from the appropriate committees and other respected church members not on these committees. The session was to be an informal think session about future options for the church. The pastor did not come to the meeting with answers, but with what all good leaders must have—the right questions. Instead of beginning with statements of positions as if debate were the task, the pastor focused the discussion on finding solutions by asking questions: What are we trying to accomplish (mission)? What must any solution accomplish (what do people have a right to expect)? What do we want to make sure we preserve with any solution (values)? Quickly the conversation turned to the ultimate goals that the group shared, and these provided the framework to assess options for handling the growth.

Resistance to change within organizations is never as simple and one-dimensional as it may seem to the leader seeking to be a change agent. There are normally technical, political, and cultural reasons for organizational resistance to change.[19] Rosabeth Moss Kanter's list of the most common reasons people resist change and lessons to be learned about change makes clear the importance of involving people early and thoroughly if change is to be successful.

Ten Most Common Reasons People Resist Change

1. It makes people feel out of control. People tighten up when they feel powerless.

2. Too much uncertainty. What will it mean for them? Is it safe?

3. Never heard it before. People do not respond well when asked for reaction on the spot. Always prepare the ground first.

4. It disrupts routine. The known and certain are appealing.

5. It makes people lose face. Looks as if what we did in the past was wrong.

6. It makes people feel uncertain about their competence.

7. There is a ripple effect on other people and efforts. It disrupts other things.

8. Things that are new are more work. People feel they have no reason to put in the extra work.

9. There is a chip on the shoulder from the past. People are mad at you for something else, or at the organization, or from some bad experience.

10. Sometimes the threat is real. Your great idea will hurt someone else. There are few totally positive ideas.

Ten Lessons to Be Learned about Change

1. Provide a clear picture of the change. Share the vision.

2. Allow room for participation in the planning. Leave some choices.

3. Share information to the fullest extent possible even if you do not have it all.

4. Divide change into small steps. Use pilot projects.

5. Minimize surprises. Provide advance warnings of change.

6. Give people a chance to digest ideas.

7. Make people feel good about their competence.

8. Reward the pioneer supporters.

9. Help people feel compensated for extra work. Does not have to be financial. At the minimum, acknowledge it.

10. Try to redeem losers. Let them know early.[20]

4. Strengthen others through sharing power.

Studies show that leaders make people feel strong, and in so doing they enable others to take responsibility for the group's success. Therefore, it is best to think of power as an "expandable pie."[21] Traditional management thinking promotes the idea that power is a fixed sum. If one person has more, another must have less. However, the expandable power pie concept leads to greater reciprocity of influence. The leader and the follower are willing to be mutually influenced by one another. As more power is given, more is received. The more power a leader is willing to entrust to others, the more they are willing to grant influence and power to the leader. Therefore, as others grow stronger, the leader's influence with them is increased.

Whether in staff committee meetings, board sessions or one-to-one discussion, the less the leader feels the need to direct and control, the more influence people are willing to give to that leader. When the leader communicates confidence and trust, then these are returned by others. An unusual example of this occurred once when a pastor and staff member had different ideas about how a particular program should be conducted. Discovering that the two shared very different assumptions about the program, a third person suggested that the pastor and staff member get together and discuss their differing perspectives. Each respected the other, and they generally worked well together. As they discussed this program, they were so persuasive and had such regard for each other that each changed the mind of the other. Thus, at the end of the meeting they still disagreed, but with exchanged positions.

Leaders are wrong to assume, says Worley, that power is a static commodity, an entity, which is stable in nature, concentrated in particular locations, and does not change. Rather, the power of a church to achieve its purposes and to alter the quality of its life is flexible. It contracts and expands. It is dynamic and diffuse. Power is lodged in the whole church; members have control over their piece of power and must finally give consent, time, ideas, energy, and money.[22]

One has to be very careful here in the use of language. Language about sharing power and empowerment can easily lead to the assumption that leaders have power and others do not. In fact, a strong case can be made for the opposite. The people in a group actually have the power. They give or withhold that power based on their interest and motivation. The real question is not so much whether the leader will empower the people, but whether the people will empower the leader to be effective. In a sense, leadership is "conferred by followers."[23]

The story of the loaves and fishes should serve as a reminder to effective leaders that God's gracious power is abundant, blessing us with a surprising extravagance. Thus, leaders will spend their time not in concern about ever-scarce power, but in reminding groups of their own extraordinary resources and power.[24]

Mary Parker Follett talks about the part of "the led in leadership." She points out that in no aspect of the subject of leadership is there greater discrepancy between theory and practice. Part of the task of the leader is to help others participate in her or his leadership, she says. The best leader knows how to make followers feel power themselves, not merely acknowledge the leader's power. And if the followers take part in leadership, it is also true that there must be "followership" on the part of leaders. There is a partnership of following.[25]

It is important to remember that all are leaders. True leaders understand that, at different times (often within the same day), a person functions as leader, follower, and peer. Earlier the story from Mary Parker Follett was told about the new school teacher having difficulty not only following, but even understanding, the leadership role of the school custodian. This is a splendid example of how all of us find ourselves in the multiple roles of leader, follower, and peer. It is true that "generalized power is virtually nonexistent in our pluralistic society."[26] To say someone "has power" is an incomplete description. People have various kinds of power.

5. Communicate.

DePree reminds us that just as any healthy relationship requires honest and open communication, so the relationships within organizations improve when information is shared accurately and freely. He adds that the best way to communicate an organization's values is through behavior, and that such communication happens all the time. Thus, communication through behavior needs to become a way of life. DePree says, "Everyone has a right to, and an obligation for, simplicity and clarity in communication. We owe each other truth and courtesy, though truth is sometimes a real constraint, and courtesy inconvenient."[27] In all communication it is helpful to remember Robert C. Neville's admonition regarding preaching. "Preaching," he says, "is not what the preacher intends but what the congregation hears."[28]

Communication not only serves to share common interests and values, it also serves to articulate what is happening and why it is happening. Thurman Arnold said, "Unhappy is a people that has run out of words to describe what is happening to them."[29] Leaders are those people who define reality in understandable and sensible terms.

Listening is one of the most important components of communication. Nothing can substitute for a live leader listening attentively and responding informally. Wise leaders, Gardner says, are continuously finding ways to say to their constituents, "I hear you." As Woodrow Wilson put it, "The ear of the leader must ring with the voices of the people."[30]

In his book, *The Human Side of Planning,* David Ewing contends that "few efforts damage the human side of planning more than errors in communication." To persuade effectively, he says, a manager must "communicate generously."[31]

Listen and *communicate* are two important words for leaders. Some would describe the leader of any group as the chief information officer. Rich dividends will come to leaders who carefully plan how to get information and feedback and how to give information accurately.

Church leaders have many vehicles to communicate information and values. Some include newsletters, bulletins, announcements, sermons, letters, staff meetings, committees, introductions, welcomes, and recognitions.

There are also many avenues for listening and receiving feedback in a local church. Some include surveys, focus groups, neighborhood group meetings, staff, discussions of various programs, and incidental conversations and comments. Each leader will discover other means both for communicating and listening.

At the seminary, I meet throughout the school year with small groups of students. In addition to getting to know one another better, we spend the bulk of the time with two questions. First I ask what they have experienced at Saint Paul that is so good they hope it remains. Then we focus on what suggestions they have for improvement. I listen and take notes. Once a month these affirmations and suggestions are distributed to all faculty and staff. This procedure may suggest similar approaches for other ministry settings.

It is a temptation for leaders to want to avoid "bad news" or criticism. The poet Audré Lord cautions, "What you know may hurt, but what you do not know may kill." Wise leaders find ways to hear both good news and bad.

6. Be with the people.

Sheer presence is essential for effective leadership. It is extremely difficult, perhaps impossible, to be a leader without generous presence, time, and attention with the people who look to you as the leader. That presence will take many shapes, forms, and expressions.

Helen Doohan shows how Paul's leadership was successful when he was "personally and intimately involved with the community and his life was intimately bound together with the life of the church."[32] On the other hand, Richard Bondi describes Paul's struggles in Corinth: Paul's very absence and the letters he sent in his place became divisive issues and gave credence to those who challenged Paul's leadership. Although Bondi argues that leaders must remain "on the edge" in order to lead, he acknowledges that leaders must have an active presence within the community to claim solidarity with it. His conclusion is "there is finally no substitute for our personal presence."[33]

A bishop recalls traveling with another bishop across the latter's home region to lead Bible studies. The local bishop had been gone frequently. He had just returned from an episcopal visit to another country, and during a question-and-answer period someone said, "We know you love the people of the country you have just visited, but do you love us?" The bishop recalling this incident said there was a moment of stunned silence. Then came an articulate and caring response to this question from a bruised and hurting person.[34]

One can manage from a seated position, but not lead from such a position. "Management is what you can do with your hands; leadership must be done with your feet."[35] One important reason that leadership requires ongoing presence with the people is to avoid isolation. Isolation is a danger for all leaders. Henry Ford, for example, was so out of touch with what was happening at his company that he could not imagine his workers voting for a union. Every leader who has lost touch with the heartbeat of followers has known a similar experience.

Those key persons who comprise the team, those without whom the vision cannot be realized, need the leader's presence. It is also necessary for all the stakeholders within the organization.

Review your calendar and do an analysis of your schedule. What does it say about your goals, priorities, and commitments? Pay special attention to those with whom you are spending time. Who is included? Excluded?

Now think more specifically about where and when you are present, seen, and available. Whom are you with, or seen by, or available to in these times? What changes can you execute to make yourself more present to those for whom you are not now present? How can you arrange to be more present for more people and in ways that fit your calling, responsibilities, and priorities? What are appropriate ways that you can be present with and for children, youth, church school teachers, older members, volunteers, staff?

Presence is never one-dimensional. At different times the involvement takes on different meanings, such as formal work on business matters, social interactions, symbolic presence, and information sharing and receiving.

When an old woman accosted the Roman emperor Hadrian, he brushed her aside, saying that he was too busy. She replied, "Then you're too busy to be emperor," whereupon he stopped and listened to her.[36]

7. Recognize people.

A good leader makes heroes out of many people. It is well to remember the admonition that "innovations sometimes succeed best when they have no obvious author."[37] It is also well to remember the place for legitimate and deserved recognition of those who make progress possible.

"If people feel they will benefit from your success," says Rosabeth Moss Kanter, "they will help you." She goes on to advise, "Share the glory as well as the work."[38] That is a good word for any who would be leaders. Constantly recognize in appropriate and specific ways the contributions of others. Let any recognitions that come your way as leader come from others. Remember that the leader's primary recognition comes in the inner knowledge that the effort is being faithful to its calling and responsible to present needs.

A pastor made it a habit each December 31 to write letters to the officers of the church expressing appreciation for their particular contributions to the leadership of the church in the past year. He mailed the letters so the people received them immediately after the beginning of the new year. Later in his ministry during a term of service in a denominational position, this pastor spent some Sundays visiting churches he had served in the past.

In one church that he had served as a young pastor many years before, a member came up to him and said, "I still have the thank-you letter you wrote me when I was a trustee. That is the only such letter I have ever received." The pastor found his remark and the very fact that he had kept the letter quite remarkable. This member had been a trustee when there was quite a bit of tension between pastor and trustees about an inadequate parsonage. It seems that this human touch of recognition and thanks by the pastor had a far more lasting impact on the church member than the differences the two of them had experienced.

8. Develop others.

David L. Bradford and Allan R. Cohen in their book *Managing for Excellence* present the model of the leader as developer in contrast to the more prevalent heroic model of leadership.[39]

The heroic model has a long history. We see a clear example in the story of Samuel, who pondered with God how to answer the people's longing and demand for a king. Having just saved the Hebrew tribes from attack by the Philistines, God interpreted the yearning for a king as a rejection of God's authority and guidance, according to Samuel. The prophet tried to dissuade the people.

The people refused to listen to the voice of Samuel and said, "No! but we are determined to have a king over us, so that we also may be like other nations, and that our king may govern us and go out before us and fight our battles" (1 Samuel 8:19*b*-20 NRSV).

The heroic model places the leader at the center of all action with responsibilities squarely on her or his shoulders. The leader parcels out work, sets objectives, monitors performance, and fixes whatever is wrong.

Even when the leader seeks input and delegates important tasks, the underlying assumption is that the good leader has the total knowledge of the situation and the responsibility for achieving success. This is a very heroic way of viewing leadership.

The heroic model of leadership is a byproduct of how organizations mythologize their leaders. It also reflects the tendency in American culture to romanticize certain heroes, making them wiser, purer, and grander than they ever were or were even capable of being.

One pastor responded to lay concerns about what was for them a complex and confusing church school literature order form by taking over the ordering of literature. This pastor also used this heroic approach in other aspects of ministry as well. A few years later when another pastor came to this church, she found church school lay leadership uninformed about what literature was being ordered, what the needs were, or what were the available options. A more helpful approach by the first pastor would have been to arrange times with the laity to go over the order form, options, and needs. At first they might have completed the order form together with the goal of developing such understanding by the laity that little or no assistance would be needed in the future.

Finally, the heroic model of leadership is a self-defeating model. The more successful one is in living out this heroic model, the more others will expect of the leader. Such success will cause others to take less initiative and not develop their own adaptive powers.[40] Most followers are willing to let leaders develop and promote their programs. However, in their minds they always see these as the projects of the leader and not their own.

The heroic model of leadership perhaps is found more often in the local church than in other organizations. It is a temptation for every local pastor. No matter how small or large the church, life revolves around the pastor in ways uncommon for leaders in many organizations. That truth came home to me when I went from a local church pastorate to seminary administration. Even though seminaries are relatively small organizations, it became apparent that one can only function effectively in that setting by being comfortable as part of a team and finding fulfillment in team success. I have since observed that there are many local pastors who can make similar transitions. There are also many who are unable to function effectively outside a system in which they are solo leaders functioning out of an heroic image of ministry.

The corrective action needed for the heroic model is not an irresponsible swing in the other direction. The leader needs to be strong and active, but in an interactive relationship with others in the organization. The developer model asks the leader to see every situation that arises as an opportunity to achieve two purposes: the accomplishment of the task and the growth and development of other people in the organization. Bradford and Cohen contend that leaders following the developer model "learn to have impact without exerting total control, to be helpful without having all the answers, to get involved without demanding centrality, to be powerful without needing to dominate, and to act responsibly without squeezing others out."[41]

Max DePree identifies at least three development roles leaders have for others in their organization: removing obstacles that keep them from doing their jobs; abandoning themselves to the strengths of others by admitting that leaders cannot know or do everything; and accepting responsibility for the identification, development, and nurture of future leaders.[42]

Leaders who give themselves to the development of others produce rich dividends for years to come. Leaders who strengthen their people create a legacy that will last. A study was conducted of the twelve executives who made up the top leadership of AT&T at a given time. It found that one key common denominator for them was that at one time each had had as supervisor one particular person at AT&T known for being a developer of persons.[43]

9. Love the people.

None of the above suggestions will work without an authentic and heartfelt love for the people. Those who would be leaders within the church would do well to see themselves as "folk theologians" in the manner of John Wesley. John Wesley became known as a "folk theologian" because he always began with people and their needs. As Martin Luther King, Jr., maintained, "Whom you would change you must first love."

Richard Baxter in the classic *The Reformed Pastor* expressed it this way:

> The whole of our ministry must be carried on in tender love to our people. We must let them see that nothing pleaseth us but what profiteth them; and that what doeth them good doeth us good; and that nothing troubleth us more than their hurt. We must feel toward our people, as a father toward his children: yea, the tenderest love of a mother must not surpass ours.[44]

When I was a pastor, I once asked why a group of people in the community who were so committed to certain issues were never present when the struggles about those issues had to be addressed. Someone replied with the devastating words, "They love the issues but not the people." Are there ways that people in your church know that you love them? Many pastors achieve remarkable success in their ministries, often in the face of major obstacles, because of the solid rooting of their work in demonstrated love for their church members. To the amazement of many, a white pastor in Mississippi was able to stay at his rural church for many years after signing a highly controversial civil rights declaration in the early 1960s. The people knew he loved them.

Robert C. Neville speaks of a common misconception of Christian leadership. On the one hand, a Christian leader must be out in front; and the more needed the leadership, the farther in front the leader needs to be. On the other hand, leadership is not leadership at all if it loses contact with others. "If no one is led," as he puts it, "there is no leadership, however strident the call to press forward."

Dean Neville rehearses the all-too-familiar stereotype of the recent seminary graduate in a first appointment. The first Sunday the pastor preaches an introductory sermon saying, "Like you I am anxious, confused, and depressed. Like you I was abused as a child. I too neglected my children and then drove them away by making them live my life. Only during my divorce did I accept my vulnerability and decide to enter ministry." The next Sunday this unhealed wounded healer returns to the pulpit with the social gospel, informing the congregation that their racism is exceeded only by their sexism, that they are too mired in the old ways of thought to recognize the evils of ageism, that the well-intentioned barbecue to welcome the new pastor was an egregious display of speciesism, and that the fellowship hall is not wheelchair accessible. Dean Neville acknowledges that this is a stereotype and that even the stereotype contains important dimensions of the Christian witness. But the message that the new pastor is communicating, far more strongly than the content, is a lack of love for the people. It is a lack of the kind of love that seeks to know and understand the people and what has brought them to this point in their Christian pilgrimage, as incomplete and inadequate as it may be. "Only leadership that establishes contact with those to be led," Dean Neville concludes, "can succeed as leadership."[45]

It is not enough to be right. For those of us engaged in ordained ministry, the real test is not primarily our own intellectual and ethical purity; the real test is effective ministry. That means being responsible to the people with whom we minister, "people God has given us" as Martin Niemoller spoke of it.

In a "Peanuts" comic strip, Schroeder is playing the piano, oblivious to his admirer, Lucy. She finally says to him, "Do you know what love is?" Schroeder stops, immediately stands and says, "Love, noun, to be fond of; a strong affection for or attachment or devotion to a person or persons." He then sits down and resumes playing the piano. Lucy looks away and says, "On paper, he's great."

INTERACTIVE APPROACH TO LEADERSHIP

An earlier section discussed the relationship of leader and group members, describing a continuum from authoritarian to laissez-faire, and the Managerial Grid with its extremes of authoritarian leader and the "country club" manager. An unspoken false assumption in those models limits their usefulness in describing pastors and congregations. The false assumption is that as one moves on the continuum or grid toward the authoritarian position, the pastor becomes stronger and the laity weaker. When the movement is in the other direction, laity become stronger and the pastor becomes weaker. A good example of the fallacy of this assumption is the story told earlier: the church known for its lay leadership stressed the key role of the pastor when laity described the work of their church.

What we should seek is an interactive approach, in which pastor and people are strong at the same time. The Approaches to Leadership Matrix, which is based on an organizational model used by consultant H. Rhea Gray, seeks to delineate such an approach.

APPROACHES TO LEADERSHIP MATRIX

Responsiveness to Others

	Low	High
Low (Identity and Values)	Passive	Reactive
High (Identity and Values)	Proactive	Interactive

The "identity and values" component of the matrix refers to one's own beliefs, priorities, ideas, convictions, and sense of direction. The "responsiveness to others" component refers to the beliefs, priorities, ideas, convictions, and sense of direction of others within the church. It also includes the felt needs of the people. In addition, it includes responsiveness to what is happening in the external environment in which the church functions.

When a pastor is low on both identity/values and responsiveness to others, the result is a passive approach to leadership. This approach tends to be found most often in bureaucracies. One hopes not to find it within the church, but examples certainly come to mind. The pastor who essentially has quit, but is still going through the motions, fits this model. That pastor has no great agenda to push, and does not particularly care about what interests the people either.

More common are the reactive and proactive approaches. When a pastor is low on identity/values and high on responsiveness to others, this leads to a reactive approach to leadership. Here the pastor is consistently seeking to please the people and do what appears to be needed, but without reference to purpose, mission, and values.

When a pastor is high on identity/values, and low on responsiveness to others, the result is a proactive approach to leadership. The proactive pastor is always and immediately clear and articulate about what is right and what needs to be done. There is, however, little sensitivity to the ideas and feelings of the congregation, or to the circumstances of the external environment.

The ideal is the interactive approach, in which there is a high regard both for the pastor's identity/values and responsiveness to others. With the interactive approach, pastor and people are strong together. The interactive approach allows everyone to win. They win, not necessarily on every issue, but on the more important matter of how everyone is regarded, treated, and valued within the life of the congregation.

An illustration shows what these approaches might look like in an actual situation. Here is the scene. Between church school and worship on a Sunday morning, a church member comes up to the pastor and says, "Last Sunday we were away visiting our daughter and her family. We went to church with them, and during the service they had a wonderful time called the children's sermon. The pastor called all the children down front, had a brief 'sermon' (it was really better than the real sermon later!), had a prayer, and then the children returned to their families. We should do the same thing here." How might the pastors described on our matrix respond? Here are some possibilities:

Pastor Reactive: During the announcement time that Sunday Pastor Reactive says, "Next Sunday we will begin a new program for our children known as the children's sermon. So, boys and girls, be sure to be here next Sunday morning." Five weeks later Pastor Reactive is accosted in the hallway before the worship service by a prominent member of the congregation who is obviously upset. The church member says, "I have been a member of this church for over forty years, and nothing has caused me so much anguish as that so-called children's sermon you have been doing. I thought worship was supposed to be for everyone. Inclusive, I believe, is the word. Now we start separating people. What do you plan to do next? Have a special time for old people, fat people, liberals? Why stop with children?" That Sunday during the announcements, Pastor Reactive says, "As you know we have been conducting an experimental program for the last few weeks called the children's sermon. While today is the last Sunday for that special program, we will be having some other special programs for children across the remainder of the year with more information about those being available later."

One can criticize Pastor Reactive for not having a personal sense of what worship is about, but it is hard to fault responsiveness to others!

Pastor Proactive: Pastor Proactive's immediate response to the church member suggesting children's sermons was quite different. "Yes, I am aware that some of my colleagues are doing such things in their worship services. However, I must tell you that as long as I am pastor here there will be no children's sermons as a part of our worship. There is no historical or theological basis for such. I will not violate the liturgical integrity of the Christian church for some passing fad that people think is cute." The church member responds, "Thank you, pastor," and leaves.

One can criticize Pastor Proactive for serious insensitivity to the feelings of a member of the congregation, but one can hardly criticize Pastor Proactive for not being in touch with personal ideas and values.

Pastor Interactive: Instead of giving an immediate answer, Pastor Interactive might seek to continue the conversation with some questions. "Tell me about the children's sermon. Have they done it long there? Did you notice what the other people in the congregation were doing during the children's sermon? What did your grandchildren say about it? Did your daughter or her husband comment on it? What impact did it make on the service as a whole?" Pastor Interactive might continue, "All of that information is helpful. In fact, you are not the first person who has suggested that we consider a children's sermon. Several have brought the idea to me and the worship committee. To be quite honest, the worship committee is divided over the matter. I, myself, have mixed feelings about it. You are aware that the worship survey we conducted last month is part of an effort by the worship committee to take into account what people in the congregation think. The committee is also studying about the history and theology of worship as they develop for us the order of worship we will use in the immediate future. I am not sure if a children's sermon will be a part of the suggested order of worship, but I will be happy to take your comments to the committee and get back in touch with you once a decision is made. Also, after six months of using the new service, the worship committee will be conducting a major evaluation. Whatever is decided in the coming weeks will be open to review later."

My guess is that when Pastor Interactive calls this church member to give the decision of the committee regarding children's sermons, the response of the church member to the pastor will be a genuine "thank you." Even if the decision is negative, the church member will appreciate the seriousness with which all views have been considered. In this situation, the pastor is staying strong, not in a covert or manipulative way, but in an open and healthy manner that any church member can respect. I once thought that a dilemma of being a leader was having to say "no" to people and having to deal with their hostile reaction. What I have discovered is that people can hear "no" without difficulty; their lives are filled with such answers. What people cannot deal with is not being taken seriously. When people's feelings and ideas are honored and respected, they become free not to have to contend for victory on every matter.

There is a proactive bias in serving organizations. I have thought often about a quotation from a management journal: "Most not-for-profit organizations (whether schools, welfare agencies, or churches) tend to be dominated by a group of professionals that feel they know more about what people need than the people do themselves."

The thought in this quotation can be argued both ways. I hope the teachers who teach my children know more about what they need than my children do. I also hope those teachers consider the needs and feelings of my children. Similarly, the pastor ought to know more about many things in the life of the church because of education and experience, but it is a mistake to let that truth become the excuse for a domineering proactive approach to ministry.

People become professionals in serving organizations out of a high sense of commitment and mission. It is not surprising that we often will make our mistakes on the proactive side as opposed to the reactive. We need to be aware of the proactive bias so that, if this bias is present in us, we can compensate; we can give more deliberate attention to being responsive to others and to the environment. If not modified, the proactive bias can finally be fatal to both leaders and organizations.

Pastors also are tempted at times toward a reactive approach or a kind of country club management (as described earlier).

The interactive approach to leadership holds within it, in dynamic tension, the strengths of both the proactive and reactive. Hence it is generally the most effective approach for pastors. It is not intended, however, to be the only approach to leadership. It should serve one well for as much as 80 or 90 percent of the time, but there is that time when a proactive approach is essential or a reactive approach becomes necessary. There are for all pastors those "here I stand" moments when one's integrity or the mission of the church is at stake. Those do not come along nearly as often as most pastors think they do, but they do arise and become pivotal moments for one's ministry. Then there are those times when a faithful pastor decides to follow the reactive approach simply to save energy for another day.

Helen Doohan, in describing Paul's "interactive path of leadership," quotes James MacGregor Burns: "[for successful leaders] . . . the wants and needs, the aspirations and expectations of both leaders and followers [are important]. And the genius of leadership lies in the manner in which leaders see and act on their own and their followers' values and motivations."[46] It is a fallacy that leaders must sacrifice their individuality for the sake of the whole. What is required is that one's views and values be reconciled with those of others, but never abandoned.[47]

The approach one chooses in relating to others will be the most important determinant of success in building a strong and broad team of key leaders and stakeholders. Ronald A. Heifetz and Riley M. Sinder explain that the mark of leadership is the guiding vision; the means of implementation are interactive.[48]

Effective leadership always takes place with the people. Leadership begins with the way you *think* about those with whom you work and serve. As a leader you are already halfway to success when you can come to see every person in the church as a strategic ally or partner.[49]

Fixed hierarchical systems of relating and leading simply do not function as they once did. We think in changed ways today of relationships such as teacher and student, employer and employee, parent and child, and spouses within a marriage. Partnership is an informing value and model for relationship and leadership. Partnership takes into account the wider social context within which leadership must function, as well as the interactive dimension of relationships and leadership. Letty M. Russell is helpful in describing an understanding of partnership that is based not on equality of gifts, but on a relationship of trust and mutuality. This partnership makes possible both service and the maximum affirmation of persons. The result, according to "God's strange arithmetic," is that the total is indeed greater than the sum of the parts. That is what good leadership is about.[50]

Rosabeth Moss Kanter expresses it this way: "The new kind of . . . hero . . . must learn to operate without the might of the hierarchy behind them. The crutch of authority must be thrown away and replaced by their own ability to make relationships, use influence, and work with others to achieve results."[51]

EXERCISES

1. What vision is emerging for your church as the appropriate vision for the immediate future?

2. Given this particular vision, who are those without whom this vision cannot become a reality? What will each need from you as leader in motivation and support for the vision to be fulfilled?

3. Who are the various stakeholders (groups with similar interests and needs) within the church? What does each have a right to expect from the church?

FOUR

CULTURE

Thinking is easy, acting is difficult. To put one's thoughts into action is the most difficult thing in the world.

Goethe

On a hot July day in 1953, the founders of the famous Menninger Clinic, Dr. C. F. Menninger and his sons Karl and Will, signed their names to a remarkable document that was "to be opened only in the event of the death of all three of us." It was a message—twenty-two pages of typed script—to the staff and trustees of Menninger. For thirty-seven years this document rested in the vault of the Menninger business office until the death of Dr. Karl Menninger on July 18, 1990.

One of the many important statements in this document was, "A certain spirit develops in an organization, and this spirit has a kind of immortality all its own." What moved the Menningers to create this unusual document and to include this statement? Reflecting upon the founding of Menninger in 1925, Dr. C. F. Menninger said, "We had the *vision* of a better kind of medicine and a better kind of world."[1]

The Menningers understood the necessity for a powerful and compelling vision. They also understood that once a vision is established, it is imperative that an ethos develop within the culture of the organization that can sustain, support, and extend the vision. It is essential to find ways to symbolize the vision and its values, and to incorporate them within the culture of the organization.

The church consultant Lyle Schaller talks about the importance of a pastor giving attention to matters of culture immediately upon arriving at a new church. Schaller understands that once a new vision emerges, there must be new structures to support that new vision, and one must make sure that traditions, values, customs, and habits are consistent with the new vision.[2]

Webster defines the word *culture* as "the integrated pattern of human behavior that includes thought, speech, action, and artifacts." Families, organizations, and entire nations possess cultures. Culture represents the "way we do things here." It is how we behave most of the time.[3] At a deeper and less visible level, culture represents the "values that are shared by the people in a group and that tend to persist over time even when group membership changes."[4] Denham Grierson in his splendid book on church culture, *Transforming a People of God,* uses culture to refer to the unique shape, flow and style of a local congregation. It means the patterned way of life produced by a people through which its members are formed and shaped by the manner of their belonging.[5]

Terry Deal says, "Culture is a concept that captures the subtle, elusive, intangible, largely unconscious forces that shape a society or a work place. It is a potent shaper of human thought and behavior within organizations and even beyond its boundaries. Culture provides stability, fosters certainty, solidifies order and predictability, and creates meaning."[6]

Every congregation has a unique culture. Worley makes a helpful distinction between the manifest culture and the latent culture, both of which are present in every church. The manifest culture is a set of perspectives on areas of congregational life such as mission, maintenance, and social interactions. These perspectives are quite apparent to the congregation and openly shape the life of the church. The latent culture is a set of perspectives on congregational life that lie dormant until an event or crisis evokes them in a manifest form.[7]

Some elements of a church culture that Worley names are congregational beliefs; patterns of relationship between clergy and laity, leaders and clergy, and leaders and members of the

congregation; and leadership styles transmitted from one generation of leaders to another. Culture may also include how people
dress, the correct way of worshiping, how church buildings are fur-
nished and used, and how a congregation deals with conflict or
does not deal with it. Everything that makes up the fabric of congregational life is a component of the culture. As the anthropologist
Clifford Geertz notes, "Whatever else modern anthropology asserts
. . . it is firm in the conviction that persons unmodified by the customs of particular places do not in fact exist, have never existed,
and more important, could not in the very nature of the case exist."[8]

It is within the culture that the vision and values come alive.
Culture is to vision what a movie is to the script. Most leaders
assume that change comes about without changing the culture.
But the vision must be incorporated within the culture before
any significant change can take place. Giving attention to culture is essential.

As perhaps the most pivotal locus for change, culture also represents the most emotion-laden and potentially conflictual
dimension within the life of an organization.

NEED FOR PASTORAL UNDERSTANDING
OF CULTURE

"The 'church' so talked about in seminary is neat, tidy, and
generally civilised. A particular congregation is never neat, sometimes barely Christian and only rarely civilised."[9] What Grierson
describes dramatically is the "culture shock" that often occurs
when a student enters a local church as pastor for the first time,
or when a pastor moves from one congregation to another.

One story illustrates the kind of cultural insensitivity some pastors exhibit when arriving in a new situation. A United Methodist
pastor from Georgia claimed to have served the shortest pastorate in the history of the conference. "It was my first assignment
as a seminary graduate. I arrived in town on a Thursday and went
immediately to the church. It was an ancient building in a tiny
town in rural southern Georgia. I could not believe what I found.
The building only had two doors and one was unusable. A large,
ugly tree completely blocked the side entrance to the building.

"I could not imagine why the congregation permitted the tree to stand. It was obviously a fire hazard. The church had no emergency exit. I decided there was no need to wait. I went back to the parsonage, unpacked my chain saw, cut down the tree, cleaned up the mess, painted the door, and waited for thanks from the congregation when they realized how decisive and hardworking their new pastor was.

"It did not work out as well as I had imagined," he continued. "It seems that particular tree had quite a reputation in that part of the state. It was known as 'The Wesley Tree' because John Wesley had planted it when he visited the town long ago. The congregation was not the least pleased with me. In fact, it was less than a week later the district superintendent thought it might be a good idea to transfer me to another congregation."[10]

The task of pastoral understanding and engagement is threefold for Grierson. The first step is to name the culture of a particular congregation. The second is to interpret what is identified. The third is a process of remaking—to use the possibilities for change and growth, which have been called "openings for ministry."

The pastor's method for understanding a local church culture is critical. Grierson offers the model of participant-observer as one that honors what the congregation is.

The participant-observer model assumes that an analysis is suspect if it is not shaped by the symbols of the people being studied. The most honored interpretation is the interpretation the people themselves place on what is studied. The participant-observer gains knowledge by taking on the perspective and style of those studied, and attempts to recreate in her or his own imagination and experience the thoughts and feelings that are in the minds of the people. It is through a process of symbolic interpretation of the experienced culture that the observer works with the data and discovers meaning in them. To insist that the interpretation be subject to the culture's self-understanding is to make an effort to overcome the perceptual bias that observers bring to an alien community.

Grierson offers the following guidelines for understanding the role of participant-observer:

1. The participant-observer shares in the activities and sentiments of the people. This involves face-to-face relationships and direct contact with the shared life.

2. The role of participant-observer requires both a necessary detachment and personal involvement.

3. The participant-observer is a normal part of the culture and the life of the people under observation. He or she does not come as an expert, but rather as a learner who, in order to learn, participates in the life of the people.

4. The role of the participant-observer is consistent within the congregation, so that no confusion is created by unexpected changes of behavior or alternating of roles.

5. The participant-observer has as a target a symbolic level of meaning in the life of the congregation that cannot be gained from observing external behavior alone, as would be the case for a detached observer.[11]

WHY IS CULTURE IMPORTANT?

Some understand what needs to be done within an organization. Others understand the culture of the organization very well. However, few people understand both what needs to be done and the cultural context together. Change and culture must work in tandem. If brilliant strategy does not have a healthy culture to carry it, the strategy will not work. On the other hand, the strongest culture cannot implement an impossible strategy.

There is inevitable frustration when leaders try to make significant change by rules, policies, and statements. These leaders expect to make major changes externally without addressing the internal heart of the organization reflected in the culture.

One reason culture is so important is that people never make judgments about organizations, including churches, on the basis of an objective assessment of reality. People do not have enough information to make objective judgments. They make judgments based on perceptions that bear some resemblance to reality. Those perceptions are most powerfully communicated through the images and symbols of the culture.

Therefore, one cannot be concerned only with the reality, but one must also be concerned about perceptions. One must give attention to the symbols and images that are being conveyed through the culture. This effort does not take away from mission, but enhances it. It advances the organization, and it also saves it from the deployment of energy, time, and resources needed to deal with negative perceptions.

An airline survey illustrated the power of perceptions. From the earliest days of airline research, people have named safety as the most important consideration in selecting an airline. One might assume that airlines need only be concerned about their safety records, which are carefully monitored and published by the government. Yet the airlines quickly learned that the "reality" of safety alone was not enough for people to view an airline as safe.

One survey was particularly revealing. It asked people at the conclusion of their flight to rank the airline on several factors, including safety. During the flight half the people sat at seats where the serving tray was perfectly clean. The other half had a serving tray with a coffee stain. Those with the coffee stain gave the airline only half as good a rating regarding safety as did those who had a clean tray. On the one hand, the cleanliness of serving trays has absolutely nothing to do with airline safety. Yet there was a connection for people who make decisions about airlines on the basis of their perceptions of safety.

A recent example of the power of symbols occurred when two pilots of a major airline were intoxicated while on duty. The incident made the national news and, more devastatingly, became the subject of countless jokes. That airline could have a superior safety record and still be helpless to convince the public of their reliability in the face of such a powerful negative image.

Emerson said, "All I have seen teaches me to trust the Creator for all I have not seen." The question before every leader is whether what people are seeing is giving them confidence in what they do not see, or instead is raising questions.

Erving Goffman says that in all communication there is information that is "given out" and information that is "given off." Leaders in the church may find it useful to ask, "What is being given off through the culture of your church? What is being given off by you as a leader? Does it lead to confidence or doubt?" When our first two children were young, I found a book about George Washington that the children thought was wonderful. On each page there was a brief story about an incident in George Washington's life, a picture to color, and a place for a large stamp that was to be found at the back of the book. Each night the children listened to me read the story so that, after the story, they could take turns coloring the picture or affixing the stamp that went with that particular story.

When we finished the book weeks later, I suggested that we talk about what they had learned from the book. They looked at each other as if to acknowledge that they knew this moment would come eventually. Reluctantly they participated. I asked them what they had learned from these stories. The younger of the two immediately replied, "I learned you have to ride a lot of horses to be president of the United States." I did not understand. None of the stories mentioned horses. Then I realized that most of the pictures contained horses. What our young daughter had "heard" was actually what she had seen.

Søren Kierkegaard told a story about a circus that set up just outside a town. The circus tent catches on fire, and a clown, already dressed for a performance, runs into town to summon help. The people think the clown is merely performing and do not respond. Kierkegaard said of the people, "They heard him with their eyes." Such hearing with the eyes is going on all the time.

Worley maintains that the church is a profound moral or immoral expression by its very existence. The church in its existence and being, even apart from its rational activities of preaching and teaching, has a significant impact upon the thinking of people. Members create mental images (perceptions, feelings, and knowledge) of the church as they *experience* the church. Worley points out that we tend to think that the church's message is conveyed only in words, but the reality is that everything a person experiences is conveying powerful meaning in addition to the words.[12]

A pastor was in a controversy with the church over the children's ministry. This church had a long tradition of a strong children's ministry in which they took great pride. Now the people were ready to ask the pastor to leave. They believed that during the current pastor's five years of service, the children's ministry had declined dramatically. The pastor was very upset over this controversy and the possibility of having to leave because of it.

The pastor could not understand their concern. The statistics were impressive. There were more programs for children, and more children were participating in every aspect of the church's life than when the pastor came. These statistics, charts, and graphs had been presented to the appropriate committees and boards; yet "the facts" made no difference to the people. They had made up their minds that their cherished tradition of children's ministry had been compromised.

An outside person then had conversations with some of the people to uncover what was going on. It was true that the children's ministry, including the children's music ministry, was growing. But the tradition of having one of the children's choirs sing once a month at the largest worship service had been abandoned. The people, most of whom had no children or grandchildren in the children's ministry, had lost their one important symbol of children's ministry. The reality had improved, but the leaders had given inadequate attention to finding ways to symbolize that reality.

Leaders of churches need to remember that congregations have personalities and cultures just as all organizations do. Furthermore, values are more caught than taught. The culture of the church is the most powerful instrument for both education and change.

ELEMENTS OF CULTURE

"Culture's primary function in organizations," according to Terry Deal, "is to give meaning to human activity." The elements of culture are important as tangible expressions, representations, and symbols of deep, unconscious thoughts and assumptions. People become attached to the elements of culture as the foundation of individual and collective meaning. When cultural elements change or are changed, people experience loss and react in much the same way as they would to the death of a spouse or the loss of a home.[13]

1. Language
Language is a crucial element of the culture of any organization. Grierson asks: What are the key words and phrases used by the people to describe their life together? What are the dominant images shaping congregational life?

In discussing the place of language in a congregation, Grierson makes a distinction between outer speech and inner language. Outer speech is largely descriptive, technical, or denotative. It has a measure of objectivity implicit in its use and can be detected in formal and colloquial conversation. Generally it is what we call public language. Inner language, by contrast, is interpreting language that confers meaning on significant events. It is the language of understanding that unveils the hidden layers of the structure of experience. It is feeling language, personal language, the language of crisis. It is committing language that requires a stance toward the reality to which it makes testimony. There is also the distinction in any congregation between speaking language and nonverbal language.

Perhaps most important, according to Grierson, is that in every congregation there is a circumscribing imagery that shapes the life of that congregation. A congregation gains its strength from the pervasiveness of its shared images. An overarching idea can be sustained by such images and embody a fundamental vision of the people's shared existence.[14]

2. Space

Space says much about the life and values of a congregation. Grierson points out that space is capable of bearing properties we ascribe to people. It can be warm or cold, open or closed, light or dark, welcoming or menacing.

When we order space, it communicates, in the very design, our view of what is important and what is not. "To discern the value ascribed to spatial reality by a congregation," Grierson says, "and to appreciate the symbols that are cherished by the people, is a way of moving closer to the centre of their shared life."

Most important for Grierson is that the category of space, when employed in dialogue with the people, "can uncover a thousand secrets. The institutionalized order and organised arrangements people give to their way of being together is capable of telling the hidden tale of their spiritual pilgrimage."[15]

Architecture and physical space communicate a great deal about an organization. They send messages about priorities. One pastor concluded, for example, that the church's efforts to build community were seriously hampered because the sanctuary had seven doors that were made for quick entrance and exit, but did not make possible any common gathering area.

You may find it helpful to do a "space audit." Survey your church facilities asking the question, "What messages are being communicated by our physical facilities?"

CULTURE

I have often used the following exercise with seminary students: Imagine moving to the community in which your local church is located and attending your church as a visitor for the first time. Put yourself in the position of the person new to the community and the church. What would you be thinking? What would you be doing? What would it be like? Physically go through the motions of arriving, parking, going in, sitting down, opening the bulletin, going through the service as if it were actually happening, and then leaving. Take notes on your feelings and observations, especially what you learn about your church that you did not know before.

This exercise emerged out of my own experience as a pastor. I put myself in the position of a new person arriving for the first time at the church I was serving. I then realized what powerful messages, many of them negative, were being given off by the physical surroundings. For example, a newcomer would normally come first to the 11:00 A.M. service instead of the earlier service. They would need to park in one of the far-away parking lots because the others would already be filled by persons attending church school. Thus some would receive their first negative message, "You are welcome here if you are physically able to walk that long distance from the more distant parking lots."

As the newcomer approached the church, other such messages would appear. The physical environment was also saying, "You are welcome here if you know which of the many doors to enter . . . if you know where the nursery is . . . if you know where the restrooms are . . . if you are able to climb steps. . . ." Some simple changes (reserved handicapped parking and simple directional signs to the sanctuary, nursery, and restrooms) addressed some of those issues.

3. Symbols

Paul Ricoeur has said that every revolution is first a revolution of our guiding images.[16] The root meaning of the word *symbol* is to unify and to focus. "To understand the significant symbol or symbols of a people is to know much about them," Grierson says. "For the meanings of a community are stored in the symbols they indwell. The symbols represent a level of reality that says, 'this is the way the world is.' It is the cluster of sacred symbols woven into some sort of ordered whole that is determinative for the view of the world held by those who participate believingly in that to which the total configuration points." In the words of Mircea Eliade: "The symbol reveals certain aspects of reality . . . which defy any other means of knowledge. Images, symbols, and myths are not irresponsible creations of the psyche: they . . . fulfill a function, that of bringing to light the most hidden modalities of being."[17]

Although a church building may be filled with symbols, not all of them are significant for the people. "Only those which strike a chord in the present experience of the community can truly be said to be significant at this point in their journey. What is meant by significant is the symbol's direct connection to present identity, its living influence on what is believed and done by the people."[18]

4. Rituals

The drama of organizational life is most clearly seen through its rituals. While such rites take on different forms, they always serve to symbolize and bring to life the values, hopes, and dreams of a people. Deal reminds leaders: "Ritual is never imposed; it arises naturally. Leaders can convene occasions and encourage symbolic transformations; they cannot make them happen independent of the collective will."[19]

Culture must be ritualized if it is going to thrive. Without expressive events and rituals, any culture will languish or die. In the absence of ceremony or ritual, important values have no impact. Those who would be leaders often miss the point and overlook the benefits of focusing on the ritualistic aspect of day-to-day organizational life.[20]

There is no religious faith that exists without rituals of some kind, "for the function of rituals is to give concrete expression to what is believed." George Santanyana argued that there must be specific rites and specific myths that give meaning to the rites. No one can be religious in general.

"In the rituals and symbolic gestures of a people," Grierson says, "the world as lived and the world as believed and imagined are fused together. Word and act become one event. And at the heart of that coming together is the fundamental confession of the people."[21] Acts, gestures, rites, and rituals tell us who we are and what we should do, and they shape ways of behaving within an organization. The rituals must not only be present, but they must be consistent with the values being proclaimed. If the signals sent through the rituals are mixed or contradictory, then the rituals carry no power toward accomplishing the vision.

5. Heroes and Recognitions

Every culture or tradition lives by the compelling stories of its heroes. We tell the stories because in so doing we are able to appropriate the central hope of our present pilgrimage. They act as exemplars for us, paradigms of faith, in which by memory and repetition, we shape our lives by their example.[22]

Heroes personify those values and epitomize the strengths of an organization. Heroes are pivotal figures in a strong culture. When people become weary in pursuing the vision or are tempted to abandon it, the memory or current example of heroes will often call people back to the vision.

Deal and Kennedy describe the impact and importance of heroes as follows:

1. They make success attainable and human.
2. They provide role models.
3. They symbolize the organization to the outside world.
4. They set a standard.
5. They motivate others.[23]

Effective leaders make heroes of many persons, but only of those persons who embody the vision and values being pursued. Leaders are looking for persons who act in heroic ways to support the vision and values. They find appropriate ways to acknowledge, recognize, and celebrate these persons and their examples. To honor them is much more than a personal recognition. It is a way of bringing the entire group closer together around shared commitments, and a way of reinforcing the seriousness and priority with which they take the vision and values.

The role of the leader in such recognitions is, according to Kouzes and Posner, to focus on key values, make recognition publicly visible, and be personally involved. The most important honors are reserved for those people who preserve the integrity of the vision more than their own desires. These are the genuine heroes. These are the heroes who will continue to live and have influence for years to come in shaping the life of the group—if leaders are perceptive enough to recognize them.

6. Daily routines

"Do not forget," wrote Teilhard de Chardin, "that the value and interest of life is not so much to do conspicuous things . . . as to do ordinary things with the perception of their enormous value."[24] Jesus told his disciples not to be anxious, but to consider the quiet simplicity of wildflowers blooming and dying in a field.

People pay great attention to your daily actions and activities. Be sure that these actions are reinforcing the vision, values, and priorities that are central.

Which meetings do you attend or not attend? What work priorities do you focus upon? In what issues do you become personally involved? All of these daily actions send signals to the church about what is important. Are they reinforcing or undercutting the vision and values you are articulating?

A revealing example of cultural differences within two apparently identical organizations occurred during a discussion at our family dinner table one evening. My wife teaches at an elementary school; our son attends another elementary school in the same school district. They began talking about lunch procedures at their schools. One would expect that everything would be the same since both schools operate under the same program and policies. However, what emerged during the conversation was a fascinating example of how the two school cultures had developed differently regarding this matter.

They talked about the role of teachers in the process, the role of the cafeteria workers, the role of the students, the time of day when lunch choices were made, the nature of the report that went from the teachers to the cafeteria, and flexibility. It was as if they were talking about two schools hundreds of miles apart. As each described her or his own school's procedures, the other would often respond by saying, "That would never work in our school," or "Our teachers would never do that," or "I do not see how you make that work."

Each school had taken the same policies and stayed within those guidelines. But each had developed a sense of ownership and workability using very different procedures that fit the people and circumstances of their schools.

7. Cultural Network
   The characters that Deal and Kennedy say make up the cultural network of organizational life are:

   Storytellers—people who define and change reality by telling the stories of an organization.
   Priests—people who "worry about the religion (of an organization) and keeping the flock together."
   Whisperers—the powers behind the throne.
   Gossips— the "troubadours of the culture."
   Secretarial Sources—people to whom others often talk first and in most detail.
   Spies—people who are liked and have access to many different people in the organization.
   Cabals—two or more people who secretly join together to plot a common purpose, usually to advance themselves in the organization.[25]

   Think about your church. Are any of these players present in your church? Are all of them? Try identifying people in your church who serve each of these purposes in the cultural life of your church. These are the people who make up your church's cultural network.
   Deal and Kennedy offer the following suggestions to work with the cultural network:
1. Recognize its existence instead of feeling above it.
2. Cultivate a key network of contacts, especially the key storytellers and priests.
3. Treat every person with whom you have contact with the same deference you would reserve for the most important person in the organization. Remember that each person has many roles and contacts that you do not readily see. To some people, if only family, and often to many, each person is important, one to whom at least some others look for credible information about you and your organization.
4. Ask people you meet to explain the meaning of things. Ask them about history.

5. Ask each person about other people with whom you should talk.
6. When you find the storytellers, cultivate a special relationship with them.[26]

It is important to remember that most communication occurs through the cultural network. It is here that opinions are shaped and attitudes developed. Formal communication methods, important as they are, are successful only when there is an alignment between them and the communication going on through the cultural network. If the two means of communication are at odds, then the messages going through the cultural network will always get through and be dominant.

Leaders will do well to remember that the culture of an organization provides the most important lever for genuine and long-term change. Any change that does not engage the heart of a culture is superficial at best and will not last long if it ever takes hold at all. It is within the culture that much of change takes place.

ROLE OF THE LEADER

1. Role model

The willingness of the leader to live the vision is absolutely critical to effective leadership. The key question for the leader is, "Are you willing to wear the vision in the same way that people wear clothes?"

It is amazing how many people are watching you as leader. It is surprising to discover how many and what stories and tales they are telling about you. Whether you realize that people are watching you, or whether you know what stories they are telling, both realities are always present. The question is not whether that is taking place, but whether you as leader are behaving in ways consistent with the vision and values you articulate.

Leaders can influence cultures far beyond what most leaders imagine. However, many leaders make little positive impact because they say one thing and send contradictory messages through their behavior. Behavior is the key.

Words show the wit, but actions meanings, according to Ecclesiastes. Or as Richard Baxter advised clergy centuries ago: "Take heed to yourselves, lest your example contradict your doctrine, and lest you lay such stumbling-blocks before the blind, as may be the occasion of their ruin; lest you unsay with your lives, what you say with your tongues; and be the greatest hinderers of the success of your own labours."[27]

2. Storyteller

Do you as leader talk without embarrassment about the vision and values? Do you tell the story with emotion and passion? Most effective leaders are adept at the use of language and tell the story of the mission, values, and vision in clear and fresh ways. The leader is the "evangelist for the dream."[28] Richard Bondi puts it this way: "Leaders hear powerful stories and tell them to those they would lead. In the process they find inspiration for their own leadership and offer destinations to people of restless hearts."[29]

Robert W. Lynn describes the role of a seminary president in ways that fit the role of a pastor. He talks about the teacher/leader role. He believes that it is impossible to be a true leader without being a teacher. The teaching/leading emerges out of the vocation of the organization, its history, future possibilities, and the different publics of the organization.

Leaders give people a story through which they can organize their values and hopes. The story becomes a rallying point for those committed to the mission, vision, and values.

Early in my ministry in Philadelphia, Mississippi, I used an illustration in a sermon that proved to be decisive for the future of my ministry there. I referred, almost as an afterthought, to a conversation I had had the week before with an African-American pastor from another state. The pastor had indicated that he and his family would be traveling through Mississippi that summer on vacation. I told the congregation that I had invited the pastor to worship at our church while they were in Mississippi. I reported to the congregation the pastor's response: "Are you sure we will be welcome at your church?" I said I had told him, "You need to realize that things have changed in Philadelphia, Mississippi. At First United Methodist Church everyone is welcome." What I was doing was lifting a vision. That vision did not represent where everyone in the congregation was at that time (and some of the people took the opportunity to remind me of that!). However, in the coming months and years, characterized by great change and movement to a more inclusive ministry and congregation, that vision gave many people the story around which they could organize what was happening. When people from other congregations would make negative remarks to them about what was happening at First United Methodist Church, they had a story to tell. They would simply say, "At First United Methodist Church everyone is welcome."

3. Grand gestures

A grand gesture is a bold and memorable act that exemplifies dramatically the vision and values. It may not be an earthshaking action, but it calls attention to itself in a special way. The leader just showing up for (or missing) a particular occasion can be a grand gesture. A telephone call at a particular moment can be a grand gesture, or the placement of a leader in a particular position. An act of graciousness when the opposite is expected can be a grand gesture. Grand gestures communicate boldly a leader's commitments, and they remain in the minds of people.

Grand gestures are important, make an impression, and are remembered. A loyal elderly member told a pastor about her son who was seriously ill in a hospital many miles away from the rural community in which the pastor was serving. He went to visit her son. Seven years later the son died. When his wife saw the pastor at the funeral, she immediately recognized him and said, "Thank you for coming to see my husband in the hospital."

A leader may have the beliefs and intentions, but without grand gestures these commitments will never be stamped clearly on the minds of people. A leader uses sensitivity, intuition, instinct, and judgment to know when grand gestures are called for and what grand gestures are appropriate to convey the right values. Effective leaders never miss an opportunity to reinforce and dramatize the central values and beliefs of the culture.[30]

Holding to one's vision and values when all circumstances seem to call for the opposite is indeed the grandest of gestures. At the 1976 Democratic National Convention, the Reverend Martin Luther King, Sr., gave the benediction. The noted journalist Haynes Johnson described it this way: "Here he was, a man who has suffered as much grief as anyone should have to endure—his son, Martin, assassinated, his wife insanely murdered while playing 'The Lord's Prayer' on the church organ, his youngest son drowning in his swimming pool—an old black man from the Deep South preaching about reconciliation and faith and love."[31]

4. Moments of truth

Moments of truth refer to how leaders react to critical incidents. They are teachable moments. If they are missed as opportunities for leadership, they cannot be recaptured. Proper timing is essential. To miss such a teachable moment is like missing a cue in a play. The message about what counts in the organization is "delivered, demonstrated, pointed out, and emphasized by the leader's moments of truth."[32]

"Making an appropriate response while in crisis is the acid test of leadership." According to Art McNeil, "Playing the part is easy when things are going well. But once the shooting starts, you soon find out how good leaders really are. That's why practicing your signalling skills on a daily basis is so important. Appropriate responses must become second nature; they need to become so ingrained that in the face of challenge, your response will always be compatible with and supportive of your organization's vision and values."[33]

The effective leader is looking for every opportunity to communicate and reinforce vision and values. Carlyle Marney used to speak of the "Messiah coming around the corner." The leader is always confronted with opportunities that call for clear words and actions consistent with vision and values.

How one responds moment by moment to the values and sensitivities of other people represents important moments of truth. Occasionally people will come to the seminary to speak or to interview for a position and will use terminology or make statements that simply do not fit. It is clear immediately that they have not given thought to the mission, history, and values of the context in which they seek to be taken seriously. When this insensitivity happens, one can immediately feel how uneasy everyone becomes. Yet, some of the students who are bothered because their community values are not respected may return the following weekend to the churches they are serving and make the same mistake.

One pastor reports that he feels he never overcame a mistake he made within his first month in a new church. In a small town in western Kansas there was a community event held one weekend each year sponsored by the church. It brought together the church, larger community, and former residents as no other occasion did. At an early board meeting during his tenure he referred to the event as "that thing you do."

In Gloria Naylor's novel *Mama Day,* a preacher gets in great difficulty shortly after his arrival when he tries to stop a local custom dear to the people. Wise Mama Day assesses the preacher's action: "When you open your mouth too much, something stupid bound to come out."

We often see the negatives in a new ministry setting quickly, but not necessarily the positives. For example, special events may appear to be a waste of time until we realize how much meaning those events carry. Worship practices or music preferences may seem undesirable and inadequate. Ways of organizing and carrying out the ministry of the church may seem inefficient. It is normally wise to wait before being publicly and casually critical of current practices. The practices may need to be changed, but the skillful leader will make sure that the values and meaning current practices carry will be cared for after the change.

5. Day-by-day routines and actions

The leader must focus on those two or three priorities that will make the greatest difference over the long term. The leader must also understand that genuine change comes not by one or two dramatic actions, but by a thousand small things done day by day. Studies of the significance of daily activities of leaders conclude that leaders need to practice what the organization preaches on a day-to-day basis and encourage others to do the same.

It is well for leaders to audit their daily actions to see what they communicate and to see how consistent with vision and values those actions are. Use of time is one of the best places to begin. Does one's time usage reflect priorities and values?

Monitoring one's reaction to critical incidents and how one gives feedback about mistakes is often quite telling. One of the most important areas to monitor is what questions the leader regularly asks. Leaders often do not have the best answers, but leaders must have the correct questions. Another area to watch is what one rewards and recognizes. By the same token it is well to ask what it is you as leader challenge and correct.[34]

What information do you need? What information do you ask for? Someone has said that what is inspected, not expected, tends to get done. One pastor with a large staff has a "charts day" once a month when they examine together certain statistical charts. This regular action makes it clear to everyone what is important enough to be monitored.

A business leader developed a worldwide reputation after concluding that it was not realistic for his company to be 100 percent better than the competition. But it was realistic for them to become 1 percent better in a hundred different ways. As Adrienne Rich says of freedom, "It isn't once . . . freedom is daily, prose-bound, routine remembering. Putting together, inch by inch, the starry worlds."

Another issue at stake in day-by-day actions is integrity. A church secretary once told me about working with a pastor who had a public image for caring and compassion: "What you see is what you get. Everything she presents in public I see everyday in all the work we do together."

6. Work the network

Personal involvement with people is essential. A leader must be with the people being led. Talk of "working the network" does not refer to a calculating or antidemocratic approach to leadership. It simply recognizes how communication and change occur within any organization. They take place within the cultural network of groups and relationships.

One pastor of a very large church has a monthly luncheon discussion with a group of people who are key leaders and influencers in particular groups within that large congregation. They differ in many ways, but what they have in common is that they are close to the pulse of major segments of the church and are respected by those people. This particular discussion group focuses only on worship, but the concept could be used in many different ways. Such personal involvement does not take away at all from normal organizational structures. For the leader it supplements those by providing direct and regular feedback from the people most involved.

7. Learn to dance

While the culture must carry change, there is always a tension between the existing culture and change. Effective leadership requires patience, flexibility, and tolerance for ambiguity. "Leaders need to think about how they can convene, encourage, and become active participants in rituals, social dramas, and healing dances as a means of transforming modern organizations," according to Deal. He says that leaders need to be both directors and actors to move effectively from the breach caused by change to reconciliation. He suggests that those who manage change in modern organizations need to learn to dance. While changing and managing are incompatible in his view, "dancing and changing may be complementary: the change requires the dance; the dance transforms the change."

Leading change in a local church has become for many pastors a joyless and burdensome responsibility. Learning to dance may help. As Deal reminds us, "Heart will not be restored by knowledge; it can only be restored by dancing and healing."[35]

The cultural life of the church illustrates that good intentions, noble objectives, a just cause, and enthusiasm are not enough. A leader needs to be what Saul Bellow described in *Henderson the Rain King* as a person who is "no mere dreamer but one of those dreamer-doers." It is within the culture of the church that much of our "doing" will take place if the dreaming is to become a reality.

In their studies of what followers most want from leaders, Kouzes and Posner found three basic categories: commitment, competence, and consistency. These qualities not only must be present with the leader, they must also be communicated regularly and clearly to people through the culture of the organization.

While I was a local church pastor, before beginning any formal study of leadership, I concluded that there were three things necessary for a particular change to take place within a local church. In those days I worded the sequence in this way: articulate the vision, find ways to symbolize the vision, and then make sure the vision is a reality. It is amazing to me now how those conclusions, based almost purely on my day-by-day experiences as a pastor, are verified by more systematic studies of leadership.

There is a local church in which the membership and the church staff are warm and caring, but one only comes to know and experience this care in times of great loss. For most people these crisis times do not come often, so the majority of this congregation never experiences the tremendous effort that is made every day to care for people. There are no symbols or other ways of communicating this caring spirit. People in this church, therefore, become inactive, and others never choose to join because the culture communicates distance and coldness, despite all of the fine efforts at caring most do not see. People never have enough information to make objective judgments based on reality. People must depend on the perceptions they receive from the culture to make their judgments and decisions. This is a reality with which pastors and others in local churches must deal.

Symbolizing the vision through the culture is crucial. One can articulate the vision and the vision may become real to some extent, but the vision will never take hold until it takes hold in the various dimensions of the organization's culture.

The theme of the Evanston Assembly of the World Council of Churches in 1954 was "Jesus Christ—The Hope of the World." In preparation for the assembly twenty-five "leading theologians" from around the world met ten days each summer for three years. They prepared and presented papers on the theme, and the results of their work were published. But who remembers that work?

There was also a hymn contest in conjunction with the assembly. The winner was "Hope of the World" by theologian Georgia Harkness. Who remembers it? Millions of Christians around the world know and sing this marvelous testimony of faith. How do we find vehicles that not only declare the truth, but actually convey the truth into the culture of the church in powerful and lasting ways?

When we speak of the culture of the church, we are talking about the church becoming a living model of God's vision for the church as the body of Christ in the world. The calling to ministry is a calling to be a part of a great vision. The greatness of ministry is not found in the church structure or in our particular assignment, but in the greatness of the vision given to the people of God.

Letty Russell talks about our living now as if the world were already on its way to what God intends. We know what God intends for the world so we can go ahead and begin acting on those intentions here and now. We as the people of God are called to live as if the world were as God intends; therefore, we help the world live its way into a new future.

The writer of Ephesians describes the way in which God has made Jews and Gentiles one community in the church. The church then is a model for what God intends for the whole world. As remarkable as this unity is, it is but a glimpse of what God intends for the whole world. As amazing as this unity is, it is only a sign of what can happen in the whole of creation. It is as if God is saying, "If this can happen, there is no limit to what is possible."

How marvelous it would be if the church could become that kind of model. If people wanted to see where there is perfect peace, then they could look at the church. Where there is justice, look at the church. Where categories of race and class that matter so much to the world mean nothing, look at the church. Where there is neither male nor female, but all are one in Christ Jesus, look at the church. What a great vision we have!

EXERCISES

1. How would different people in your church respond to the question, "Tell me about your church?" What do their responses tell you about the church? From what aspects of the culture of your church do these perceptions come?

2. When someone comes to your church for the first time, what will they see, hear, and experience? What does this communicate to them about your church's values? Will the church's stated values be reinforced? Contradicted?

FIVE

INTEGRITY

People must think of us as Christ's servants, stewards entrusted with the mysteries of God. What is expected of stewards is that each one should be found worthy of [this] trust.

1 Corinthians 4:1-2 JB

I ntegrity is an issue today in all fields. The arena that seems to receive the most attention is politics. Mollie Ivins, the irreverent critic of Texas politics, tells of a well-known figure in Texas who was recently indicted again. This time the charge was not reporting all conflicts of interest. The public official's excuse was that on the form on which he was to list all of his conflicts of interest, he ran out of room on the page. Ivins's comment was that this man is not a crook, but he is "ethically challenged."

Today leaders in almost every profession are being found to be severely ethically challenged. There is a "contemporary crisis in the professions" in which the lay public is challenging both the competence and dedication of the professional class.[1]

The ethical challenge within the church has known no distinctions. It has involved leaders at every level of the church, persons from every denomination, and persons of many different theological and social perspectives.

What has been the response of the church? One group of

observers of professional ethics among clergy has found that clergy have made minimal responses to these developments. The literature gap on the subject of clergy professional ethics is revealing. There were many books in the 1920s and 1930s, and then there was an almost total absence of literature until the late 1980s and early 1990s.[2] These are not easy times for clergy. Recent events have brought a genuine questioning of influence, role, identity, and appropriate behavior.

In one sense, this has always been the case. Notice how clergy identity and behavior have been the objects of negative stereotyping—on television, in the news media, and even by great writers. Remember J. D. Salinger's character Holden Caulfield complaining that all the preachers he ever heard spoke with "Holy Joe" tones? He could not understand why they did not speak in their natural voices. Or, do you remember the line from John Updike's *Rabbit Run*? "He is getting slightly annoyed at the way the minister isn't bawling him out or something; he doesn't seem to know his job."

Unfortunately, the issues today are more serious than ministerial monotone or judgmental preaching. The church and its leaders have proven not to be exempt from the failures of recent years when integrity has been the key issue in government, business, and the church.

Religious leaders have paralleled other discredited public leaders. Too often we have seen the same patterns—advocacy of social policies for others with which they themselves are unwilling to live, greed and love of money, failures of personal morality, and one-issue zealotry. The examples are numerous and painful. This era is hardly the first time that this has been the case for religious leaders, but it is a reality of our time of which we must take account.

We do not expect clergy to be exempt from the human struggles of our time; however, we could have hoped for a qualitatively different response from them. The church and the world do not expect absolute purity, but they can expect acknowledged standards of integrity and a reasonable way to respond to failures. If we are honest, we must recognize that this pattern has diminished the capacity for leadership by the churches in our society. At the same time, it has made ordained ministry less inviting.

Integrity has to do with both organizational integrity and the personal integrity of the leader. As A. Bartlett Giamatti has reminded us, leadership is essentially a moral act. In a sense all real leadership is values-driven leadership. The key to effective leadership, then, rests not only on those values and directions that shape and focus leadership, but also on the constancy of the organization and leader in living out those commitments. Integrity has far more to do with consistency between articulated values and behavior than it does with adherence to some prescribed code.

In a book on integrity and business, the authors describe the quest for integrity as an effort that is at once moral, philosophical, and practical; it strives to achieve coherence among daily actions, personal values, and basic aims of the organization. The consistency that leaders seek in the quest for integrity is not the use of a cookie cutter or a rigid rule for decisions and actions. Integrity means that the same personal values and organizational aims will powerfully influence what a person does and says.[3]

A biographer's description of Dorothy Day provides a superb example of integrity as coherence and consistency. "It was not what Dorothy Day wrote that was extraordinary, nor even what she believed, but the fact that there was absolutely no distinction between what she believed, what she wrote, and the manner of life she lived."[4]

Hannah Arendt put it well: "Power is actualized only when word and deed have not parted company."

VALUES-DRIVEN LEADERSHIP

When one begins to read the literature of leadership, one soon discovers that there is no way to talk about leadership apart from values. Consider a writer such as John W. Gardner, who has written so eloquently on leadership through the years. Notice the words that tend to recur: spirit, will, hope, faith, and beliefs. Notice also the words used in one study of extraordinary business leaders in America to describe common characteristics found among them: vision, meaning, trust, self-worth, and affirmation of others. During the civil rights movement Martin Luther King, Jr., called upon his followers to do more than register and vote. He called them "to create leaders who embody virtues we can respect, who have moral and ethical principles we can applaud with an enthusiasm that enables us to rally support for them with confidence and trust."[5] A concern for integrity, character, and values does not go uniquely with church leadership. It goes with effective leadership.

I continue to be amazed at the power of personhood in determining the effectiveness of a leader. In the school where I serve, nearly all the students are in graduate degree programs to prepare to serve in local churches. During their theological education, they will gain much knowledge and will develop skills that will allow them to function as competent professionals in ministry. However, the strongest determinant of their future leadership will be who they are as persons. This cannot take the place of the learnings and skills, but it will be the most powerful factor in their long-term development as leaders. I sense this is true for every other kind of leadership.

The Watergate governmental scandal presents a classic example of leadership uninformed by the personal value of integrity. One of those involved, Jeb Stuart Magruder, spoke, I am sure, for many colleagues in the words he addressed to Judge John Sirica: "Somewhere between my ambitions and my ideals, I lost my ethical compass."

Just think how different our national history in that era would have been if anyone associated with those events had had a functioning, operative, and lively sense of right. Judge Sirica said that just a little honesty and a little character would have stopped the whole awful thing at the outset.

Over twenty years ago Eudora Welty spoke of integrity in connection with the task of the writer as "integrity that can be neither lost nor concealed nor faked nor quenched nor artificially come by nor outlived, nor, I believe, in the long run, denied." Seldom do we value or even try to understand, until it is too late, those of unswerving loyalty to principle. If we did, we would reserve our highest honors for those who say with Job, "Till I die, I will not violate my integrity."

Therefore, integrity is an essential element in leadership in the church. What is at stake is not so much the public image of a profession, but the very effectiveness of our ministries.

THE PASTOR AS MORAL LEADER

"Whatever else a minister is, at the heart of her or his vocation is the call to be a moral leader," says Richard Bondi. "The overriding question of Christian ministry is not *whether* leadership will arise. It is, rather, *what kind* of leadership will arise and where it will lead the Body of Christ."[6]

Sara Little, in her search for ways to address the critical need for leadership, found help in the concept of "experiments with truth" associated with Gandhi. It confirmed her conviction that leadership has to do with morality and religion and education. She reminds us that at the heart of James MacGregor Burns's theory of leadership is the concept of moral leadership that concerns him most. Burns maintains that this moral leadership, which he calls transforming leadership, "is a relationship of mutual stimulation and elevation that converts followers into leaders and may convert leaders into moral agents."[7]

Pastors face both the temptation not to lead and, as Bondi says, the temptation to betray their essential calling to be moral leaders. Robert F. Kennedy highlighted the power of individual moral action and leadership in a 1966 speech in South Africa:

> Each time a person pursues an ideal or acts to improve the lot of others or strikes out against injustice, he or she sends forth a tiny ripple of hope, and crossing each other from a million different centers of energy and daring, those ripples build a current that can sweep down the mightiest walls of oppression and resistance.

PERSONAL INTEGRITY

One crucial aspect of clergy professional ethics is personal integrity and trustworthiness.

When lay persons are asked what they want most in pastors, the characteristics that rank highest always are those that describe the pastor as person. As important as competence in the skills of ministry may be, it is the personal character of the pastor that laity name as most significant. Pastors must be persons in whom people can put trust.

Laity of one mainline denomination were asked in a national

survey, "What values (personal traits and characteristics) do you look for and admire in a pastor?" The descriptive words most named, well ahead of all other named characteristics, were *honest, caring,* and *cooperative.*[8]

A more comprehensive survey across many denominations a decade ago found that the most important factors in personal leadership are (1) the degree of service without acclaim, (2) personal integrity, and (3) Christian example. David S. Schuller, the survey director, says that issues of pastoral functioning emerge as important only after these personhood issues have been established. He goes on to identify the most detrimental factors in pastoral effectiveness as (1) self-serving ministry, (2) undisciplined living, and (3) emotional immaturity.[9]

Martin E. Marty has said that clergy often complain of living in a fishbowl. Marty says that this concern is misplaced. His observation is that when people quit showing interest in your life, then you are in trouble. This statement is not meant to justify prying eyes that seek to invade appropriate privacy, but it is to say that lack of interest on the part of laity is a sure sign that one is no longer looked to as a leader.

James T. Laney, president of Emory University, has called upon the so-called learned professions of medicine, law, teaching, and ministry to recover a keen sense of "being honorable," for each relies upon a profound sense of honor for its fulfillment. Each profession meets the person with whom it deals at a point of need. That person relies not only upon the judgment and wisdom, but also upon the sense of honor, of the professional person.

"To be a professional, after all," according to Rebecca Chopp, "is to have responsibility for making decisions and judgments that require a certain character, principles, and commitments." In addition, recent studies of clergy professional ethics have made it clear that ethics for leaders in the church must go beyond character. Ethical considerations must take into account, far more seriously than we have done before, the ethical implications of the roles that we occupy as leaders in the church. We must acknowledge the inherent power that goes with such roles, even when we may feel personally very powerless.[10]

John Wesley understood this when he insisted that the moral

lives of pastors should be exemplary. Brilliance is not required for ministry, but integrity is.

Does this mean that pastors must be superhuman or manifest absolute perfection? No. Karen Lebacqz in her book *Professional Ethics* puts it this way: "This does not mean that the minister is permitted no faults. It means that the minister is permitted no faults *that have to do with trustworthiness.*"[11]

PROFESSIONAL ETHICS

A great surprise for church leaders when they begin reading supposedly secular books about leadership is that the language used in the best of the books seems to come directly from the vocabulary of the church. They expect to find elaborate grids, schemes, and designs. Instead, they find the opposite. The words that dominate have to do with values and character. It soon becomes quite evident that there is no way to talk about leadership without talking about values, meaning, and personhood. The character and values of the leader do matter. In a recent Columbia University study, business leaders rated ethics highest when asked what matters most for them. The study concluded that business leaders must be above reproach because "impeccable ethical standards are indispensable to credibility."

A term sometimes used in communication theory is the "ethical proof" of the speaker. Ethical proof refers to the credibility that the hearers accord the speaker. When the ethical proof is high, the task of persuading the audience is not hard. When the ethical proof is neutral, the speaker has a more difficult time. When the ethical proof is extremely negative, the speaker has a very difficult time persuading the audience. This concept means that the way the constituents perceive the character of the leader is probably much more important than the "facts" of the situation.

Behavior is the key to credibility. Do people perceive us as doing what we say we are going to do? Predictability becomes a key to trust. Such credibility is won minute by minute, but it can be lost very quickly.[12] Once lost, it may be impossible to regain. The task of restoring credibility is almost impossible within that particular setting of leadership.

Good leaders understand that they must use their own credibility, not the credibility of others. There is some degree of credibility that comes with any position. Predecessors have built up that credibility through hard work, and people will give to you an important degree of that credibility. However, to use up that credibility rather than credibility you have earned for yourself is finally inadequate.

An older colleague advised a newly elected bishop that he would only have as much authority as he deserved, no matter what the church law says. Or as Henry Mitchell advised a beginning pastor, "Don't use your authority until you've got it."

One key to establishing and maintaining credibility is the quality of relationships of trust that are established by the leader. Therefore, the priority for a leader is to establish a relationship of trust and respect with the people with whom the leader is working. Everything depends on this bonding.

Nanus contends that a leader without trust can accomplish little and will soon be displaced. He says that there can be no trust unless the leader is trustworthy—dependable and reliable, honest and honorable. "Those who would exercise leadership must see themselves as having undertaken a sacred trust." The people will forgive the inevitable mistakes by a leader whom they believe to be honest, fair, and trustworthy. Along with making forgiveness more likely, being trustworthy also brings one peace. One can simply sleep more easily having, as Shakespeare said, "a peace above all earthly dignities, a still and quiet conscience."[13]

Another key for credibility is for the leader to be seen as a servant of the vision of the organization. People must always understand and never doubt that your passion as a leader is directed toward what God is calling all of you as a people to be and do. Robert Greenleaf describes this task as serving the vision and always seeking a better one. This is what it means to "take the high road" of leadership. Nothing devalues one's leadership more quickly than to be seen as pursuing one's private agenda and using the church more than serving it. As a friend has put it, one can become a "walking credibility gap."

A recent study was conducted of seminary presidents in the United States and Canada who were named by their colleagues as the most effective presidents. It found that with the most effective presidents, people often found it difficult to separate the person from the mission of the seminary. It also found that the most effective seminary leaders were willing to sacrifice their personal desires to see the mission fulfilled.

Being a servant of the vision and depending on credibility and persuasion more than authority and power help make possible effective leadership. A leader maintains personal integrity as people see the leader's commitment to maintain the integrity of the vision.

Robert Greenleaf says, "Every institution should harbor able persuaders who know their way around, who are dedicated servants of the institution, whose judgment and integrity are respected, who do not manipulate, who hold no coercive power, and who, without . . . formal assurances feel free and secure."[14] Mary Parker Follett expressed it this way, "The leader gets an order followed first, because [people] do really want to do things in the right way, and [the leader] can show them that way, and secondarily, because [the leader] too is obeying. Sincerity more than aggressiveness is a quality of leadership."[15]

SOCIAL AND ORGANIZATIONAL INTEGRITY

A second essential element of clergy professional ethics is social and organizational integrity and trustworthiness.

In his book *A Gathering of Strangers,* Robert C. Worley writes about the shaping power of institutions:

> We have paid scant attention to what human beings touch, the church itself. We have scrutinized only rarely the historical forms of the church: its structure, decision-making, political and communication processes, its rewards and punishments. And we have largely ignored the consequences of these forms for individuals.
>
> If ministers are . . . ambiguous about appropriate behaviors for themselves in the congregation . . . we dare not claim that such conditions are mere defects in their character.
>
> We have not asked how institutions shape persons. We do not think institutionally, but individualistically. For this reason, when a minister is in trouble . . . , we locate the problem in the person. It becomes a personality or character problem rather than an institutional one.[16]

The character of individuals is important, but also important are structures, standards, power dynamics, and the very methods of the church itself. What a church is as an institution may very well have more impact on its own members and society than what it says to them.

Charles H. Townes, a physicist and university professor at the University of California at Berkeley, has written on the implications of the experience of science for clergy professional ethics. He points out that the strength of science "is not the perfection of individual scientists, but rather that mistakes are usually honestly recognized, examined, and rectified, first by habits of individuals which spring from acceptance of standards, and the context in which they live, and if not, then by the community."[17]

Bennis and Nanus describe four concepts of an organization:

1. **Manifest.** The manifest concept is what is on paper. It is the mission statement, promotional literature, the organizational chart.

2. **Assumed.** The assumed view of the organization is what people perceive as existing. To get at the assumed concept one does not read documents but talks to people. One simply needs to ask a member of the church, "Tell me about your church."

3. **Extant.** The extant view is what is revealed through systematic investigation. This can be obtained by having a knowledgeable person spend enough time with one's church to give an informed and relatively objective assessment.

4. **Requisite.** The requisite concept refers to the organization as it would look if it were in accord with the reality of the situation with which it exists. The requisite is present when there is a fit between vision and need, and when there is consistency among the manifest, assumed, and extant views of the organization.[18]

The goal is not so much perfection as consistency. Within an organization integrity may be defined as consistency or congruence. The ideal is to have these four views of the organization aligned as much as possible. "Rather than assume that cultures can change to some perfect state," advises Michael M. Lombardo, "it is more reasonable to assume they can change to a more consistent one."[19] Where there is lack of alignment there is confusion, and integrity is hard to achieve. Such lack of consistency (integrity) leads to weakness. A church finds strength and power when what the church says about itself, what people perceive to be the reality, and what objective observers say are all one.

Imagine a church where the slogan on the front of the church bulletin says, "In the heart of the city with the city on our heart." A visitor attending that church asks a church member at the coffee hour to describe the church, and the response is, "We care about and serve the community in which we are located." A visiting church official after working with the church says, "The most striking feature of this church is the clarity and depth of commitment by everyone to ministry in this neighborhood." In that church there is strength.

The relationship of belief and action, words and behavior, cannot be stressed too much. No matter what we say, people only pay close attention to what we do. Inconsistency is devastating.

In Arthur Miller's play *Death of a Salesman*, Willie Loman constantly brags to his friend about his two sons. Sadly, their achievements take place primarily in Willie's mind. One day the friend's son comes by work to say "good-bye" to his father before leaving for a trip to Washington, D.C. After the son leaves, Willie asks his friend why his son is going to Washington. "He's going to argue a case before the Supreme Court," is the reply. "Argue a case before the Supreme Court," Willie exclaims, "and he didn't even say anything about it." Willie's friend responds, "He doesn't have to. He is going to do it." That is a good lesson for the church. More integrity between belief and action could make many of our spoken and written words far less necessary.

During a trip I took to China in 1978, a Chinese student began to ask many questions after learning that I was a Christian pastor. How many churches are there in the United States? How many church members? How many attend church each year? After the student heard all of these statistics that seemed so large to him, especially as a percentage of the population, one could almost see the wheels turning in his mind. "Why don't you take over?" was his reply. Of course, he was thinking in political terms, but the question is a good one. If we have the people, the facilities, and the beliefs, why don't we simply bring it off? Why should we be content merely to preach, sing, and pray about what we believe? Why don't we just go ahead and bring it off, live it?

One of Alan Paton's characters says a question asked in heaven will be, "Where are your wounds?" The quest for integrity compels us to ask where are the wounds from living day by day the faith we proclaim. Wounds are a reminder to a doubting world that we do believe what we profess.

PERSONAL HOLINESS AND SOCIAL HOLINESS

Both dimensions—personal integrity and trustworthiness, and social and institutional integrity and trustworthiness—are crucial. Our dilemma is not that both are not being examined, but rather that many people seem only interested in one or the other. Both are essential and must be held together.

The late theologian and ethicist L. Harold DeWolf expressed regret that those most concerned with personal morality often show little regard for social morality, and those who are most sensitive to social injustice seem oblivious to issues of personal morality. John Wesley was right. Personal holiness and social holiness must be seen together, always.

The subject of clergy professional ethics is neither a light subject nor one that lends itself to simple or easy solutions. On his first day as president of Yale University in 1978, A. Bartlett Giamatti issued the following memo:

> To the Members of the University Community:
> In order to repair what Milton called the ruin of our grandparents, I wish to announce that henceforth, as a matter of University policy, evil is abolished and paradise is restored.
>
> I trust all of us will do whatever possible to achieve this policy objective.

Unfortunately, a memorandum from church leaders will not be sufficient to address this matter. It is too complicated and too subtle; however, it is not unapproachable. It is reasonable for us to expect that all of us working together can make a difference. We can make sure that our church is what the Evangelical

Lutheran Church in America recently described as "a safe haven" for all persons.

Badaracco and Ellsworth, from their perspective of the business world, contend, "Leadership in a world of dilemmas is not, fundamentally, a matter of style, charisma, or professional management technique. It is a difficult daily quest for integrity. Managers' behavior should be an unadorned, consistent reflection of what they believe."[20]

The call to integrity is a powerful reminder that takes us back to the very roots of our calling to ministry. The quest for integrity is nothing more than a quest for our faithfulness in our ministry. "For it is when we forget the story that called us into ministry in the first place," says Bondi, "that we place a misguided importance on our own success or failure, or on the expectations placed on us by people in a particular time and place."[21]

The words and example of Henri J. M. Nouwen should make us sensitive to the ongoing tension between worldly success and faithfulness.

> Let me summarize. My movement from Harvard to L'Arche made me aware in a new way how much my own thinking about Christian leadership had been affected by the desire to be relevant, the desire for popularity, and the desire for power. Too often I looked at being relevant, popular, and powerful as ingredients of an effective ministry. The truth, however, is that these are not vocations but temptations. Jesus asks, "Do you love me?" Jesus sends us out to be shepherds, and Jesus promises a life in which we increasingly have to stretch out our hands and be led to places where we would rather not go. He asks us to move from a concern for relevance to a life of prayer, from worries about popularity to communal and mutual ministry, and from a leadership built on power to a leadership in which we critically discern where God is leading us and our people.[22]

The calling of God to ordained and lay professional ministry is a high calling. Ministry is the most demanding and challenging of callings. It is also the most fulfilling and rewarding. When done poorly, it is a disgrace. When done faithfully and well, there is nothing more wonderful to behold. Indeed, there is no higher calling.

EXERCISES

1. What are the "stories" being told about you in your church? If someone approached various laity in your church with the question, "Tell me about your pastor?" what would they say? What would be the recurring words or phrases? How does this match your own identity and especially the themes and values you seek to affirm in your ministry?

2. Now try this exercise about your church. How would you describe your church to people who are new residents and prospective members for the church? How would you describe your church to your best friend and confidant of many years who has no connection to your church or community? How would you describe your church if, knowing you were scheduled to leave that church shortly, your denominational supervisor asked you to serve as a consultant? That is, what would be the best and most objective assessment you could make of the church so the supervisor could make the best decisions for the future? How are those three descriptions similar? In what ways are those three descriptions different? Are all three exactly the same? In what ways does this exercise help you begin to get at the issue of organizational integrity?

CONCLUSION

I am about to do a new thing; now it springs forth, do you not perceive it?

                                                    Isaiah 43:19a NRSV

In many ways this book is written for those with a conservative style and a radical heart. The radical heart keeps us focused on a vision of the future.

                                        Peter Block, *The Empowered Manager*

The church today cries out for leadership with a radical heart that will keep us focused on a vision of the future. We face a church that simultaneously lacks conviction and humility. We face a church that demonstrates a tentativeness and uncertainty about its witness uncharacteristic of its message or history. A biographer of George Whitefield described the era in which the evangelist and others associated with the Wesleyan Revival lived as a time when people begged the church to offer faith; it was also a time when the church rarely met the challenge. Some may say the same of our time.

There are many realities in the church today that are discouraging. They are well known. Our role as leaders is to point beyond the current realities to sources of hope. Among the most influential books for me in my early ministry was the journal kept by Reinhold Niebuhr during his first years as a pastor in Detroit before his teaching career. Published as *Leaves from the Notebook of a Tamed Cynic,* it contains this statement: "Realities are always defeating ideals, but ideals have a way of taking vengeance upon the facts which momentarily imprison them." Many ideals in our Christian and denominational heritages cry out to us today. They give us sources of hope for a great new stirring of commitment and conviction.

We need to hear again the ideals of sacrifice and service reflected in the traditional language of the John Wesley Covenant Service: "I am no longer my own, but thine. Put me to what thou wilt, rank me with whom thou wilt; put me to doing, put me to suffering; let me be employed for thee or laid aside for thee, exalted for thee or brought low for thee; let me be full, let me be empty; let me have all things, let me have nothing; I freely and heartily yield all things to thy pleasure and disposal."

The Faulkner quotation is haunting: "That which is destroying the church is not the outward groping of those within it or the inward groping of those without, but the professionals who control it and who have removed the bells from its steeples." We need to put the bells back in the steeples and ring out a clear and sure message of faith and hope. We need to ring out that message until every valley is lifted up and every mountain brought low, until all the crooked paths are made straight and all the rough ways are made smooth, until the lowly are exalted and the haughty brought low, and until all humanity might come to know the salvation of our God.

We need a renewal of passion in ministry. We need a ministry characterized by a passion that can only come from a compelling message and an essential mission. People will always be weary of cures that don't cure, blessings that don't bless, and solutions that don't solve. This is a great moment for a passionate ministry.

"The serious deficiencies of our times may be in prophets who are not sufficiently realistic and inspired; in seekers who are not sufficiently humble, open, and dedicated listeners; and in enough religious leaders who are strong," says Greenleaf. "As a consequence, ours is a poorly served society."[1]

For us as religious leaders to be strong enough for the task ahead, it is essential that we maintain our sense of hope and optimism. The only true and lasting source for such hope for us is in the spiritual resources of a faith rooted in the God who seeks to make all things new. Despair and weariness give way to hope and energy as we remember that our God always goes before us as a cloud by day and a fire by night. This does not mean that the future inevitably will be better, as Callahan has cautioned. It does mean that amid the pain, suffering, and tragedies that lie before us in our future, God goes before us to make all things new—inviting us to that future that God has both promised and prepared for us. "Hope is stronger than memory. Salvation is stronger than sin. Forgiveness is stronger than bitterness. Reconciliation is stronger than hatred. Resurrection is stronger than crucifixion. Light is stronger than darkness. . . . Hope is stronger than memory."[2]

We have the promise that the very power of death will not prevail against God's church. It is with the freedom and hope that comes from this faith that we seek to be leaders for the church. It is the Easter faith that makes possible our leadership.

The challenges are different today from times past and will be different tomorrow. However, the test of leadership will continue to be the real test for us as leaders of the church. If we fail this test of providing inspired, visionary, moral, and values-driven leadership, few other things will matter. We will have been unfaithful to that courageous heritage of leadership of which we have been beneficiaries. But if we succeed, the heritage of courageous leadership will be a mere glimpse of what the future will be for a strong, vital, and faithful church.

"You are not required to complete the work," Rabbi Tarphon wrote centuries ago, "but neither are you free to desist from it."

Abigail Adams in a letter to Thomas Jefferson said, "Great necessities call forth great leaders." Those of us called of God to service in the church at this moment in history face a people and a world of great necessities. May God grant us the strength and the wisdom to become great leaders.

NOTES

Preface

1. Harris W. Lee, *Effective Church Leadership* (Minneapolis: Augsburg, 1989), p. 12.
2. Quoted, ibid., p. 85.
3. Thomas E. Cronin, *The Christian Science Monitor*, February 16, 1990.
4. Gary H. Quehl, "The Inner World of Leadership," *Presidential Papers* 7 (April, 1991): 2.
5. Robert R. Blake and Jane S. Mouton, *Executive Achievement* (New York: McGraw-Hill, 1989), p. 7.

Introduction

1. James MacGregor Burns, *Leadership* (New York: Harper & Row, 1978), p. 1.
2. "MacNeil/Lehrer Newshour," July 4, 1989.
3. Robert K. Greenleaf, *The Leadership Crisis* (Newton Centre, Mass.: Greenleaf Center, 1986), p. 1. For a careful and thorough development of servant leadership, as well as for other contemporary images of ministry (wounded healer, political mystic, practical theologian, and enslaved liberator), see Donald E. Messer, *Contemporary Images of Christian Ministry* (Nashville: Abingdon Press, 1989).
4. Cornel West, "Learning to Talk of Race," *New York Times Magazine* (August 2, 1992): 26.
5. See John W. Gardner, "The Antileadership Vaccine," *Annual Report*, Carnegie Corporation of New York, 1965.
6. Sara Little, " 'Experiments with Truth': Education for Leadership," Parker J. Palmer, Barbara G. Wheeler, and James W. Fowler, eds., *Caring for the Commonweal: Education for Religious and Public Life* (Macon, Ga.: Mercer University Press, 1990), p. 165.
7. Harry Levinson, *Executive* (Cambridge, Mass.: Harvard University Press, 1981), p. 90.
8. John W. Gardner, *On Leadership* (New York: Free Press, 1990), p. 57.
9. Quoted in George Keller, *Academic Strategy* (Baltimore: Johns Hopkins University Press, 1983), pp. 43-44.

10. Gardner, "The Antileadership Vaccine," p. 11.
11. Michael D. Cohen and James G. March, *Leadership and Ambiguity*, 2nd ed. (Boston: Harvard Business School Press, 1986), p. xiv.
12. Ibid., p. xvi.
13. Robert K. Greenleaf, *The Servant as Religious Leader* (Newton Centre, Mass.: Greenleaf Center, 1982), p. 5.
14. Helen Doohan, *Leadership in Paul* (Wilmington, Del.: Michael Glazier, 1984), p. 112.
15. See Mary Parker Follett, *Dynamic Administration* (New York: Harper, 1941).
16. Max DePree, *Leadership Is an Art* (New York: Doubleday, 1989), p. 136.
17. Levinson, *Executive*, p. 145.

1. Elements of Effective Leadership

1. Quoted in Harris W. Lee, *Effective Church Leadership* (Minneapolis: Augsburg, 1989), p. 13.
2. Quoted in James D. Whitehead and Evelyn Eaton Whitehead, *The Promise of Partnership* (San Francisco: Harper & Row, 1991), p. 11.
3. Kennon L. Callahan, *Effective Church Leadership* (San Francisco: Harper & Row, 1990), p. 66.
4. James H. Davis and Woodie W. White, *Racial Transition in the Church* (Nashville: Abingdon Press, 1980), pp. 117-18.
5. Derek Bok, *Higher Learning* (Cambridge, Mass.: Harvard University Press, 1986), p. 164.
6. Robert K. Greenleaf, *The Servant as Religious Leader* (Newton Centre, Mass.: Greenleaf Center, 1982), pp. 9-10.
7. Sara Little, "'Experiments with Truth': Education for Leadership," Parker J. Palmer, Barbara G. Wheeler, and James W. Fowler, eds., *Caring for the Commonweal: Education for Religious and Public Life* (Macon, Ga.: Mercer University Press, 1990), p. 165.
8. Quoted in Warren Bennis, *On Becoming a Leader* (Reading, Mass.: Addison-Wesley, 1989), p. 16.
9. See Robert R. Blake and Jane S. Mouton, *The Managerial Grid III: The Key to Leadership Excellence* (Houston: Gulf Publishing, 1985).
10. Kennon L. Callahan, *Twelve Keys to an Effective Church* (San Francisco: Harper & Row, 1983), pp. 41-42; *Effective Church Leadership*, p. 54.

2. Vision

1. A. Bartlett Giamatti, *A Free and Ordered Space: The Real World of the University* (New York: W. W. Norton and Company, 1988), p. 36.
2. Warren Bennis, *On Becoming a Leader* (Reading, Mass.: Addison-Wesley, 1989), p. 6.
3. John W. Gardner, *Self Renewal*, rev. ed. (New York: W. W. Norton, 1981), p. 7.
4. Ibid.
5. A. Bartlett Giamatti, *The University and the Public Interest* (New York: Atheneum, 1981), p. 184.
6. Rosabeth Moss Kanter, *The Art of Innovation* (Chicago: Nightingale-Conant, n.d.), sound cassette 4.
7. John W. Gardner, *On Leadership* (New York: Free Press, 1990), p. 13.
8. Quoted in Tom Peters, *Thriving on Chaos* (New York: Alfred A. Knopf, 1988), p. 399.

9. Peter F. Drucker, *The Non-Profit Drucker* (Tyler, Tex.: Leadership Network, 1989), sound cassette 4A.
10. Warren Bennis, *Why Leaders Can't Lead* (San Francisco: Jossey-Bass, 1989), p. 111.
11. John Navone, *Theology and Revelation* (Cork: Mercier Press, 1968), p. 116.
12. Giamatti, *A Free and Ordered Space,* pp. 37-38.
13. James M. Kouzes and Barry Z. Posner, *The Leadership Challenge* (San Francisco: Jossey-Bass, 1988), p. 89.
14. Denham Grierson, *Transforming a People of God* (Melbourne: Joint Board of Christian Education, 1984), p. 120.
15. Richard N. Ostling, "Those Mainline Blues," *Time,* May 22, 1989, 94-95.
16. Grayson L. Tucker, "Enchancing Church Vitality Through Congregational Identity Change," *The Mainstream Protestant "Decline,"* ed. Milton J. Coalter, John M. Mulder, and Louis B. Weeks (Louisville: Westminster/John Knox Press, 1990), pp. 70-71.
17. Art McNeil, *The "I" of the Hurricane* (Toronto: Stoddart, 1988), p. 35.
18. Robert C. Worley, *A Gathering of Strangers,* rev. ed. (Philadelphia: Westminster, 1983), p. 81.
19. Burt Nanus, *The Leader's Edge* (Chicago: Contemporary Books, 1989), p. 106.
20. Ibid., p. 108. H. Rhea Gray's splendid work on strategic planning has informed greatly the sources of visioning section. "Effective Not-for-Profit Organizations," unpublished monograph, 1982.
21. Robert K. Greenleaf, *The Leadership Crisis* (Newton Centre, Mass.: Greenleaf Center, 1986), introduction.
22. Warren Bennis and Burt Nanus, *Leaders* (New York: Harper & Row, 1985), pp. 103, 101.
23. Mary Parker Follett, *Dynamic Administration* (New York: Harper, 1941), pp. 143-44.
24. Worley, *A Gathering of Strangers,* p. 122.
25. Max DePree, *Leadership Is an Art,* (New York: Doubleday, 1989), p. 9.
26. Kouzes and Posner, *The Leadership Challenge,* pp. 86-87.
27. John P. Kotter, *The Leadership Factor* (New York: Free Press, 1988), p. 29.
28. Robert K. Greenleaf, *Seminary as Servant* (Peterborough, N.H.: Windy Row Press, 1983), p. 62.
29. Kennon L. Callahan, *Effective Church Leadership* (San Francisco: Harper & Row, 1990), p. 78.
30. Kouzes and Posner, *The Leadership Challenge,* p. 93.
31. Grierson, *Transforming a People of God,* pp. 44-45.
32. DePree, *Leadership Is an Art,* p. 18.
33. Bennis, *On Becoming a Leader,* p. 199.
34. DePree, *Leadership Is an Art,* p. 18; Gardner, *On Leadership,* p. 112.
35. Worley, *A Gathering of Strangers,* p. 122.
36. Bennis and Nanus, *Leaders,* pp. 92-93.
37. Greenleaf, *The Leadership Crisis,* pp. 8-9.
38. David Campbell, *If I'm in Charge Here Why Is Everyone Laughing?* (Greensboro, N.C.: Center for Creative Leadership, 1984), p. 51.
39. Kanter, *The Art of Innovation,* sound cassette 4.
40. Peter Block, *The Empowered Manager* (San Francisco: Jossey-Bass, 1987), pp. 67-68.

41. James D. Whitehead and Evelyn Eaton Whitehead, *The Promise of Partnership* (San Francisco: Harper & Row, 1991), p. 108.
42. Kanter, *The Art of Innovation,* sound cassette 4.
43. The first three pitfalls are from Block, *The Empowered Manager,* p. 105.
44. Kanter, *The Art of Innovation,* sound cassette 4.

3. Team

1. James M. Kouzes and Barry Z. Posner, *The Leadership Challenge* (San Francisco: Jossey-Bass, 1988), p. 79.
2. Warren Bennis and Burt Nanus, *Leaders* (New York: Harper & Row, 1985), pp. 107, 139.
3. Kouzes and Posner, *The Leadership Challenge,* p. 131.
4. John W. Gardner, *The Chronicle of Higher Education* (January 7, 1987), 30; Rosabeth Moss Kanter, *The Art of Innovation* (Chicago: Nightingale-Conant, n.d.), sound cassette 2.
5. Peter F. Drucker, *The Non-Profit Drucker* (Tyler, Tex.: Leadership Network, 1989), sound cassette 1B.
6. James D. Whitehead and Evelyn Eaton Whitehead, *The Promise of Partnership* (San Francisco: Harper & Row, 1991), p. 211.
7. John W. Gardner, *On Leadership* (New York: Free Press, 1990), pp. 112-18.
8. David Campbell, *If I'm in Charge Here Why Is Everyone Laughing?* (Greensboro, N.C.: Center for Creative Leadership, 1984), p. 59; Gardner, *On Leadership,* p. 20.
9. Max DePree, *Leadership Is an Art* (New York: Doubleday, 1989), pp. 39-41.
10. Mary Parker Follett, *Dynamic Administration* (New York: Harper, 1941), p. 286.
11. DePree, *Leadership Is an Art,* p. 16.
12. Ibid., p. 42.
13. Ibid., p. 25.
14. Warren Bennis, *On Becoming a Leader* (Reading, Mass.: Addison-Wesley, 1989), p. 197.
15. Gardner, *On Leadership,* p. 199.
16. Michael M. Lombardo, *Values in Action* (Greensboro, N.C.: Center for Creative Leadership, 1986), pp. 7-8.
17. Follett, *Dynamic Administration,* p. 294.
18. Warren Bennis, *Why Leaders Can't Lead* (San Francisco: Jossey-Bass, 1989), p. 30.
19. Mary Ann E. Devanna and Noel M. Tichy, *The Transformational Leader* (New York: John Wiley and Sons, 1986), pp. 72ff.
20. Kanter, *The Art of Innovation,* sound cassette 6.
21. Kouzes and Posner, *The Leadership Challenge,* p. 164.
22. Worley, *A Gathering of Strangers,* p. 41.
23. Gardner, *On Leadership,* p. 24.
24. Whitehead and Whitehead, *The Promise of Partnership,* pp. 125-26.
25. Follett, *Dynamic Administration,* pp. 289-90.
26. Gardner, *On Leadership,* p. 55.
27. DePree, *Leadership Is an Art,* p. 92.
28. Robert C. Neville, "The Apostolic Character of Ordained Ministry," *Quarterly Review,* 10/4 (1990): 13.
29. Gardner, *On Leadership,* pp. 17-18.
30. Ibid., pp. 27, 29.

31. David Ewing, *The Human Side of Planning* (New York: Macmillan, 1969), p. 136.
32. Helen Doohan, *Leadership in Paul* (Wilmington, Del.: Michael Glazier, 1984), p. 59.
33. Richard Bondi, *Leading God's People* (Nashville: Abingdon Press, 1989), p. 110.
34. Rueben P. Job, "Ministry in the New Millennium: Challenge and Hope," *Saint Paul Occasional Papers,* (1990), 4.
35. Kouzes and Posner, *The Leadership Challenge* (New York: Macmillan, 1988), sound cassette.
36. Bennis, *Why Leaders Can't Lead,* p. 141.
37. Clark Kerr, quoted in Derek Bok, *Higher Learning* (Cambridge, Mass.: Harvard University Press, 1986), p. 160.
38. Kanter, *The Art of Innovation,* sound cassette 7.
39. See Donald L. Bradford and Allan R. Cohen, *Managing for Excellence* (New York: John Wiley and Sons, 1984).
40. Ronald A. Heifetz and Riley M. Sinder, "Political Leadership: Managing the Public's Problem Solving," in *The Power of Public Ideas,* ed. Robert B. Reich (Cambridge, Mass.: Ballinger Publishing Company, 1988), p. 184.
41. Bradford and Cohen, *Managing for Excellence,* p. 62.
42. DePree, *Leadership Is An Art,* pp. xix, 7, 12.
43. Robert K. Greenleaf, *The Servant as Religious Leader* (Newton Centre, Mass.: Greenleaf Center, 1982), pp. 29-30.
44. Richard Baxter, *The Reformed Pastor* (Edinburgh: Banner of Truth Trust, 1656), p. 117.
45. Neville, "The Apostolic Character of Ordained Ministry," 9.
46. Doohan, *Leadership in Paul,* pp. 58-59.
47. Mary Parker Follett, "The Process of Control," lecture delivered at the London School of Economics in 1932, in *Papers on the Science of Administration,* ed. by Luther Gulick and L. Urwick (New York: Institute of Public Administration, 1937), pp. 163-64.
48. Heifetz and Sinder, "Political Leadership: Managing the Public's Problem-Solving," p. 181.
49. Allan R. Cohen and David L. Bradford, *Influence Without Authority* (New York: John Wiley and Son, 1990), p. 17.
50. See Letty M. Russell, *The Future of Partnership* (Louisville: Westminster/John Knox, 1979).
51. Quoted in Cohen and Bradford, *Influence Without Authority,* p. 1.

4. Culture
1. *Menninger Perspective,* 1990.
2. Lyle Schaller, *The Senior Pastor* (Nashville: Abingdon Press, 1988), p. 39.
3. Terrance E. Deal and Allen A. Kennedy, *Corporate Cultures* (Reading, Mass.: Addison-Wesley, 1982), p. 4.
4. John P. Kotter and James L. Heskett, *Corporate Culture and Performance* (New York: Free Press, 1992), p. 4.
5. Denham Grierson, *Transforming a People of God* (Melbourne: Joint Board of Christian Education, 1984), p. 34.
6. Terrance E. Deal, "Culture, Change, and Loss," *MLE Alumni Bulletin,* 3/1 (December, 1989): 1.

7. Robert C. Worley, *A Gathering of Strangers*, rev. ed. (Philadelphia: Westminster, 1983), pp. 94-95.
8. Grierson, *Transforming a People of God*, pp. 85, 3.
9. Ibid., p. 18.
10. R. Robert Cueni, *What Ministers Can't Learn in Seminary* (Nashville: Abingdon Press, 1988), pp. 83-84.
11. Grierson, *Transforming a People of God*, pp. 42-44.
12. Worley, *A Gathering of Strangers*, p. 45.
13. Deal, "Culture Change and Loss," 2.
14. Grierson, *Transforming a People of God*, pp. 67-71, 117.
15. Ibid., pp. 61-62, 66.
16. See also Maria Harris, *Teaching and Religious Imagination* (San Francisco: Harper & Row, 1987), p. 4.
17. Mircea Eliade, *Images and Symbols*, trans. Philip Mairet (London: Harvill Press, 1961), p. 59.
18. Grierson, *Transforming a People of God*, pp. 106-7. A study of symbols and the American presidency is Barbara Hinckley, *The Symbolic Presidency* (New York: Routledge, 1990). "The term *symbolic* . . . should not be opposed to *real*. Symbols have reality, clearly, as a projected self is seen and perceived by others" (5).
19. Deal, "Culture, Change, and Loss," 4.
20. Deal and Kennedy, *Corporate Cultures*, pp. 59, 63, 64.
21. Grierson, *Transforming a People of God*, p. 111.
22. Ibid., p. 100.
23. Deal and Kennedy, *Corporate Cultures*, pp. 4, 39-40.
24. Belden C. Lane, "Dragons of the Ordinary: The Discomfort of Common Grace," *The Christian Century* (August 21-28, 1991), 74.
25. Deal and Kennedy, *Corporate Cultures*, pp. 87-98.
26. Ibid., pp. 101-3.
27. Richard Baxter, *The Reformed Pastor* (Edinburgh: Banner of Truth Trust, 1656), p. 63.
28. Dave Patterson ("evangelist for the dream") quoted in James M. Kouzes and Barry Z. Posner, *The Leadership Challenge* (San Francisco: Jossey-Bass, 1988), p. 21.
29. Richard Bondi, *Leading God's People* (Nashville: Abingdon Press, 1989), p. 64.
30. Deal and Kennedy, *Corporate Cultures*, pp. 142-43.
31. Quoted in James D. Anderson and Ezra Earl Jones, *The Management of Ministry* (San Francisco: Harper & Row, 1978), p. 126.
32. Kouzes and Posner, *The Leadership Challenge*, p. 201.
33. Art McNeil, *The "I" of the Hurricane* (Toronto: Stoddart, 1988), pp. 81-82.
34. Kouzes and Posner, *The Leadership Challenge*, pp. 201-5.
35. Deal, "Culture, Change, and Loss," 4.

5. Integrity

1. Dennis M. Campbell, *Doctors, Lawyers, and Ministers* (Nashville: Abingdon Press, 1982), pp. 31, 37.
2. James P. Wind, et al., eds., *Clergy Ethics in a Changing Society* (Louisville: Westminster/John Knox Press, 1991), p. 11.
3. Joseph L. Badaracco, Jr., and Richard R. Ellsworth, *Leadership and the Quest for Integrity* (Boston: Harvard Business School Press, 1989), pp. 4, 206.
4. Robert Ellsburg, *By Little and By Little* (New York: Alfred Knopf, 1984), p. xv.

5. Quoted by Robert Michael Franklin in "Clergy Politics: The Black Experience," in Wind, *Clergy Ethics in a Changing Society*, p. 281.
6. Richard Bondi, *Leading God's People* (Nashville: Abingdon Press, 1989), p. 24. The critical place of integrity for leadership in all arenas is illustrated by an article on leadership in nursing which says, "To achieve success for individual nurses and for the nursing profession, nursing needs transformational leaders who are *moral leaders* (emphasis added)." Anne M. Barker, "An Emerging Leadership Paradigm," *Nursing and Health Care* (December): 207.
7. Sara Little, " 'Experiments with Truth': Education for Leadership," Parker J. Palmer, Barbara G. Wheeler, and James W. Fowler, eds., *Caring for the Commonweal: Education for Religious and Public Life* (Macon, Ga.: Mercer University Press, 1990), pp. 166, 168-69.
8. A research project of the General Council on Ministries of The United Methodist Church and Saint Paul School of Theology. The results are available from Dr. Mearle L. Griffith, Associate General Secretary, General Council on Ministries, 601 West Riverview Ave., Dayton, OH 45406-5543.
9. See David S. Schuller, et al., eds. *Ministry in America* (San Francisco: Harper & Row, 1980).
10. Wind, *Clergy Ethics in a Changing Society*, p. 89 (Chopp). "Recent studies" include Marie Fortune, *Is Nothing Sacred? When Sex Invades the Pastoral Relationship* (San Francisco: Harper & Row, 1989), Karen Lebacqz, *Professional Ethics* (Nashville: Abingdon Press, 1985); Karen Lebacqz and Ronald G. Barton, *Sex in the Parish* (Louisville: Westminster/John Knox Press, 1991); and Peter Rutter, *Sex in the Forbidden Zone* (Los Angeles: Jeremy P. Tarcher, 1989).
11. Lebacqz, *Professional Ethics*, p. 89.
12. Kouzes and Posner, *The Leadership Challenge*, pp. 24-25.
13. Burt Nanus, *The Leader's Edge* (Chicago: Contemporary Books, 1989), pp. 96-97, 105.
14. Robert K. Greenleaf, *The Leadership Crisis* (Newton Centre, Mass.: Greenleaf Center, 1986), p. 7.
15. Mary Parker Follett, *Dynamic Administration* (New York: Harper, 1941), p. 276.
16. Robert C. Worley, *A Gathering of Strangers*, rev. ed. (Philadelphia: Westminster, 1983), pp. 28-29.
17. Charles H. Townes, "On Science, and What It Might Suggest About Us," *Theological Education* XXV/1 (Autumn, 1988): 21.
18. Warren Bennis and Burt Nanus, *Leaders* (New York: Harper & Row, 1985), pp. 50-52.
19. Michael M. Lombardo, *Values in Action* (Greensboro, N.C.: Center for Creative Leadership, 1986), p. 25.
20. Badaracco and Ellsworth, *Leadership and the Quest for Integrity*, p. 209.
21. Bondi, *Leading God's People*, p. 107.
22. Henri J. M. Nouwen, *In the Name of Jesus* (New York: Crossroad Publishing Company, 1989), pp. 71-72.

Conclusion

1. Robert K. Greenleaf, *The Servant as Religious Leader* (Newton Centre, Mass.: Greenleaf Center, 1982), p. 49.
2. Kennon L. Callahan, *Twelve Keys to an Effective Church* (San Francisco: Harper & Row, 1983), p. xx.